GODWARD

GODWARD
Personal Stories of Grace

Edited by
TED KOONTZ

HERALD PRESS
Scottdale, Pennsylvania
Waterloo, Ontario

Library of Congress Cataloging-in-Publication Data
Godward : personal stories of grace / Ted Koontz, editor.
    p. cm.
    ISBN 0-8361-9035-1 (alk. paper)
      1. Mennonites—Biography. 2. Spiritual biography. 3. Grace
(Theology) I. Koontz, Ted, 1946- .
BX8141.G63 1996
289.7′092′2—dc20
[B]
                                     95-40971
                                         CIP

GODWARD
Copyright © 1996 by Herald Press, Scottdale. Pa. 15683
    Published simultaneously in Canada by Herald Press,
    Waterloo, Ont. N2L 6H7. All rights reserved
Library of Congress Catalog Number: 95-40971
International Standard Book Number: 0-8361-9035-1
Printed in the United States of America
Book design by Gwen M. Stamm/Cover photo by D. Michael Hostetler

06 05 04 03 02 01 00 99 98 97 96 10 9 8 7 6 5 4 3 2 1

WITH THANKSGIVING

for the life of Marlin E. Miller, 1938-1994,
seminary president,
co-worker,
dear friend,
channel of God's grace to me

for the life of Leland W. Gerber, 1915-1994,
father-in-law,
photographer,
lover of beauty,
dispenser of blessing,
a window to God for me

and for the life of Winifred E. Gerber, 1916-1995,
mother-in-law,
giver of love in the small and the ordinary,
source of life for those dearest to me.

Contents

Editor's Preface

THIS BOOK is the result of an idea which came to me in the quietness of an early morning several years ago. I envisioned a book of conversion stories, transformation stories, stories of how some leading Mennonite Christians have been touched, changed, by God's gracious Spirit. The book would be a "testimony meeting." It would say that being a Christian means encountering Christ and would say this simply by telling stories of how that has happened for some of us and what a difference that has made. To those who slumber in a humdrum routine or withdraw into a mere "existing" mode because of deep wounds, the book would say, "Genuine joy and newness *are* possible!" It would confront those who are in the church but are not *really* believers with the claims of Jesus on our lives. It would tell our children that God is real and that walking Godward is walking home, into joy.

It would be a book of personal stories. Stories of initial commitments. Stories of being transformed in deep ways, even years after commitment to Christ. Stories of how what had been known in the head became life-giving in the heart. The book would speak openly about a part of our existences that—along with sex and money—we keep hidden: our personal religious lives. It would attempt to bring our deepest religious experiences out of the dark, to remove the bushel basket, to make it possible for people to see the light.

It would be by Mennonites . . . and for Mennonites. But it also would be an invitation to those outside our Mennonite Christian world to join us on an exciting faith walk toward the heart of God, toward transformation, toward being remade by the Spirit. It would be an invitation to join a community which, at its best, knows that God's grace is unfailingly and boundlessly forgiving and that as we receive God's grace, again and again, we are enabled to walk more faithfully into deeper discipleship and joy.

My being drawn to such a book is, of course, related to my own journey. I am the son of a pastor and grandson of three-and-a-half pastors; the half was my Mennonite grandmother. Unlike my United Brethren grandmother, my Mennonite grandmother could not as a woman in the 1930s to 1950s be recognized officially as a pastor, in spite of her gifts and ministry. I made early and serious commitments to Christ and, before college, a commitment to follow God's call anywhere, *even* into the pastorate if—horrors!—that was where it led.

I have clung to those commitments, sometimes in circumstances that were not easy. I recall myself as a Mennonite Christian pacifist graduate student with no political science background studying international relations and nuclear strategy in the rather worldly-wise government department at Harvard. I remember my depression that first semester as I absorbed the shock of colliding worlds. But I never left the Mennonite church.

I wanted to follow the teachings and example of Jesus. I did not believe that being Christian mainly meant seeking certain religious experiences—or lots of talk (testifying) and little walk (following). I was put off by talk that seemed to reduce encounters with God to formulas that implied that God comes to us only in certain ways, at certain times, in certain settings, and that each of us ought to be "saved" fully and finally at one specific moment. This focus on specified formulas and specified experiences left me out. I was and am, like many in our society, skeptical of a wordy, showy Christianity which often seems less than authentic.

Why then a book of grace stories—even a "testimony meeting"—of all things? Because early one morning, about a year before the idea for this book came to me, I experienced what I can most succinctly call my "Easter Sunday." How that happened is part of the story I have chosen to tell in the first chapter of this book. It was a crucial "conversion" for me. Though it did not cause me to abandon my conviction that Christian faith must include works along with words, it did convince me that we impoverish ourselves, not only when we talk too cheaply, but also when we refuse to speak of our walks with God.

Even though I had been teaching in a seminary and spoke often about theology, I did not speak readily about my personal walk with God. I preferred to let my life speak for itself. I believe now that this reluctance to speak was not mainly a reaction against seemingly unauthentic words but a cover for the fact that my faith was increasingly inadequate. My refusal to speak of my personal walk with God hid the lack of a vital walk.

I knew better theologically, but I had basically reduced Christianity to trying to do what I believed God said we should do. I was seeking to live the Christian life without really knowing God's grace forgiving my sins and healing my wounds. I was not pleased with what my life was speaking through my doing because, I see now, I was not who I wanted to *be*. Discipleship was wearing me out.

Now I believe that even if I had had a vital personal walk with God but still not spoken about it, I would have cut myself off from others on the things that matter most.

Nothing can better overcome our human loneliness than sharing with one another our personal journeys Godward.

When others and I share journeys, I usually come away encouraged by hearing how the gospel lives on in the lives of people I know—rather than only in the dusty pages of the Bible and church history or across the world (or city) in some exotic mission field. And at those moments when I feel God is nowhere to be found or my spirit sinks under the weight of heavy responsibilities, sadness, or death, sharing journeys allows others to walk with me through the valley.

My central hope for this book is that it will encourage reflection on and telling of stories—unique and varied stories, personal stories of encounters with the grace of Jesus, authentic stories that deal with the nitty-gritty of life. Nothing would make me happier than to have groups of persons gather prayerfully and expectantly, read a story from the book, then talk about how that particular story intersects (or doesn't) with the stories of those in the circle.

But in whatever way *Godward* is used, I hope the book helps readers have "eyes to see" and "ears to hear" God's coming. Perhaps that will mean recognizing, naming, and opening more grateful for God's quiet, unnoticed presence. Perhaps it will mean acknowledging an absence of God—and opening to and pleading for God's coming. Perhaps it will mean giving thanks for already knowing what the writers here testify to: God comes, and God's coming turns night to day. That is good news about which I cannot help but speak, in spite of my aversion to wordy Christianity.

Apart from my story, which is first because it is a continuation of what I have said here, the stories are arranged alphabetically. There seemed no necessary logic to them. Because God comes to us in ways that meet us each where we are, the stories are diverse. Some are life pilgrimages, some snapshots of one incident, some dramatic conversions, some gentle nudgings.

Although a strong effort was made to include contributors from diverse ethnic and racial backgrounds, the authors of the stories come disproportionately from my world of North American Mennonite academics and church leaders. Perhaps that is a disadvantage. Yet I think the stories they tell are stories that could come from many sources. And perhaps such personal stories from church "leaders" can help break down some barriers which creep in between those in Mennonite schools and other Mennonite offices and Christians who work in the "real" world. I hope so. While some of the writers are sophisticated intellectuals, the gospel I hear in their stories is much like the good news I heard from my grandmothers.

I owe a debt of gratitude to the many people who helped make this book possible. I think especially of those who contributed directly to it—the writers who have risked speaking in print of things that matter; Michael A. King, editor at Herald Press who offered encouragement, flexibility, and patience; Kevin Miller, who helped type and format the essays; and, in particular, Rachel Miller Jacobs, who in addition to being a dear friend became my trusted adviser and encourager in relation to the book and who did much of the editor's hard work of suggesting revisions and making corrections. Thanks to each of you.

My hope that I could find persons to write the sorts of stories found here has been fulfilled beyond any dreams I had that morning years ago. You will discover whether these true stories encourage you, prod you, move you Godward. But receiving them, corresponding with their authors, hearing many more stories than are printed here, seeing and sharing much Godward-leaning with various associates, making new and rich friendships—all of this has made the project good news for me. Working on it has made me more confident than ever that finally, even in the midst of much that is hard, "all is well." That confidence is a gift without price. For that gift I owe and feel inexpressible gratitude to the One who gave it, the One we know as God.

—*Ted Koontz*
Epiphany 1995

GODWARD

1

Born Again

Ted Koontz

> Jesus answered him, "Very truly, I tell you, no one can
> see the kingdom of God without being born from
> above." . . . Nicodemus said to him, "How can these
> things be?" Jesus answered him, "Are you a teacher of
> Israel, and yet you do not understand these things?"
> —John 3:3, 9-10

"ARE YOU a teacher of seminarians, and yet you do not understand these things?" It's embarrassing to say that my honest answer must be, "Yes."

In fact, for years I often smirked (only inwardly, I hope) with superiority when I heard talk about being born again. I was too sophisticated for that. But it happened to me—as a middle-aged seminary professor.

I had long been a Christian. Yet in my Christian walk, there was a nagging question—is all this God business whistling in the dark? There was another question which pressed in on my life as the years went by—is this *all* there is to life, to Christianity? And there was a weightiness about my discipleship that made it more of a burden than a joy.

My new birth came after years of studying nuclear war and after delaying parenting for a decade, partly because it seemed unfair to bring children into this mess of a world. It came after living among the poor in the Philippines. It came after walking with my father through an excruciating, losing battle with cancer. It came after all the other pains that come into a forty-five-year-old life. It came at a conference on stopping male violence against women in Colorado in February 1992, a conference I desperately did not want to attend.

I wrote in my journal the first morning in Colorado, "You know, God, that I do not want to be here. Why didn't you send the snowstorm that I joyfully heard about on the radio yesterday morning?"

I knew that I, as a white male, would be blamed for another of the world's ills, this time violence against women. I simply didn't want to hear it again, though I had believed it was true for twenty years.

Yes, men do dominate and violate women, in personal and systemic ways, and it ought to be stopped, I felt. *But why are they picking on* me, *bringing me here to beat up on me? I'm different.*

I trotted out my reasons to boast, like Saint Paul did. I wasn't macho—I'm shorter than Gayle (my wife) and less personally assertive than she is. I lectured already in 1975 about the evils of "maleness" as defined in our society— especially its violence, often directed against women. I encouraged Gayle to do seminary and doctoral work when she had doubts about her ability to do so. I was the staff person who facilitated the creation of the Task Force on Women in Mennonite Central Committee.

Largely because of Gayle's job, I left graduate school, against the advice of my professors, to move to Goshen College. I supported efforts to look first for qualified women, not men, when filling positions at the seminary. I accepted Gayle's becoming dean of the seminary where I teach and becoming not only my equal but my boss.

Naturally, this is a rather self-serving summary of my history on these issues. But it reflects how defensive I felt as I went to Colorado.

Yet I knew, when I was honest with myself, that there

was work for me to do in Colorado. My work especially had to do with my anger, an anger expressed most often to those closest to me—Gayle and our children. I did not like who I was becoming—an angry, bitter, hateful, lonely person destructive of those near me. My anger was rooted in festering wounds. I felt powerless to heal myself, to lift the weight. So I longed for, prayed for a miracle, though I did not really *expect* one. I felt weighed down by the cares of the broader world, and by my own inability to make even my small part of it right.

My journal entry that first day continued, "Since you didn't send the snow, God, I take it that you want me here. I will be overwhelmed these days—I know I need your presence. I trust you will make this a good time. When opportunities for growth come, let me seize them. Hold me this day."

The days that followed were hard but good. Many things contributed. A providential discussion about lamenting, as modeled in the Psalms, by owning our hurts, pouring out our venom, confessing our pain. Conversations in which I learned firsthand of the sexual abuse some Mennonite women have suffered at the hands of some Mennonite men. Sitting in a circle with twelve men, listening to their confessions of their worst incidents of violence against women, their patterns of abusive behavior.

Confessing there the worst incident I remembered: my yelling fiercely at Gayle and the children one evening in the car on the way home from—of all places—the seminary. Acknowledging my times of silence, coldness, my flashes of anger which made my family wary of me, perhaps even afraid of me.

Not being allowed in that circle to "explain" (and therefore justify) this abusive behavior, being forced simply to state it. I *said* what I had known in my dislike of myself but had never confessed: "I abuse those closest to me."

Confessing my sins concretely and to others, hearing others confess, being cared for through it—this was revealing, empowering, freeing, an experience of grace.

For me an even deeper experience of grace came through lamenting my hurt, my pain. Moving beyond my anger required this grieving. And it required forgiving those who I felt had caused it. I had known I needed to forgive, of course, and had tried many times to do it.

Four things were different in Colorado. First, I had been praying, in my hoping-against-hope way, about these matters intentionally for more than a year. I was prepared.

Second, strangely perhaps, I came to identify with the stories of women I heard in Colorado. By doing so I accepted myself as a victim in need of healing as well as a victimizer in need of repentance.

Third, when I could no longer bear its weight, I poured out to a friend my pain, my inability to fix things, my desire to be transformed, my helplessness in transforming myself.

Fourth, and perhaps most important, I *confessed* my woundedness, my inability to heal myself or really forgive. Yes, I told of things which had hurt me. But I told the stories in a different way. I had always connected my sinful anger with my having been hurt. By doing so I had subtly justified or excused my behavior. Now I saw *my* sinfulness more sharply. So this time (though it was not something I was consciously aware of then) instead of blaming others, I simply lamented the pain.

In retrospect, I see that a double confession was necessary for my transformation: confession of my *sin* (not explaining or misnaming or minimizing it) and confession of *my* woundedness (not blaming others for their sinfulness in hurting me). And I discovered that confession had to be made specifically and to others.

Another event made an important contribution to my

new birth. We were at worship the last night of the conference. The women facilitators asked us men to write down one thing we were willing to give up to help stop violence against women. We were then to throw what we had written into a garbage can at the center of the room. I had no idea what to write, but out of the blue it came with perfect clarity. It was something I knew would be costly and painful—though I had no idea then how costly. But I did it, and it was right.

I woke early the last morning in Colorado with deep fear grasping me. I realized I was visualizing being severely beaten because of the decision I had made the night before. But I also realized that my commitment to do it was not shaken by the fear. Gradually I found the fear receding—and I found my many burdens being lifted. I began to feel joy, a bubbling, bursting-forth joy that simply overflowed.

I went to look in a mirror to check if it was really true. It was. I saw myself smiling joyfully, broadly, happily (not happy-sadly) for the first time in years. A friend immediately saw it in my face. That morning I felt a new love welling up in me—a new love of Gayle, our children, myself, God. It was a joyful, resurrection love, not the committed, heavy, sad love of the cross I knew well. I felt powerful and good.

I *knew* for the first time with absolute certainty that God is gracious, powerful, able to make things new. I knew that the weight of pain and anger I had carried was lifted. I knew I would be less angry, less impatient, less abusive when I returned to my family. I knew I had forgiven, I knew I was forgiven, I knew I had experienced a new birth—indeed, a "new creation."

This was the miracle I had been praying for, yet not daring to expect. There wasn't time that morning to talk with the person to whom I had confessed my pain the day before, except to say "This is Easter Sunday for me. It's the morning I've met the risen Christ." I learned that being born again is possible, even for a stodgy—but in some ways worldly-wise—middle-aged seminary professor.

I have learned something else since Colorado. I need to be converted again and again. God did not finish with me that one morning. This is clear to me in many areas, and I suppose the areas where I need it most I may not yet notice. I see my need for conversion in my criticism of things that are less than perfect, especially in the church and its institutions. I am so quick to see and to say what is wrong! If anything, this fault, this sin, has grown worse since my "conversion." I now know things can be different and *right* (that is, the way I want them to be)—why aren't they? I know that this attitude, which often makes me speak a word of discouragement rather than encouragement, indicates that I need more conversion.

And though I have been better with my family, I need more converting there too, especially in relating to our children. Patterns of interaction do not change easily. Nothing has been more pervasive in my journal over the last years than reflections on being a father. Nothing seems like such a glorious opportunity, and nothing gives more joy. Yet there is nothing so truth-revealing, so humiliating, nothing which reminds me so frequently that I am not finished. Yes, conversion is ongoing. I suppose it will take longer than I can possibly live for God to convert me!

Yet something transformative did happen to me in Colorado. My inner landscape is different. Perhaps I said just what is different most adequately only two days after returning from Colorado. I was to speak in a seminary chapel service on "A Testament of Hope," reflecting on Martin Luther King, Jr., and using as my text Romans 8:18-39, where Paul roots our hope in God's ever present love. Before going to Colorado, I had been worried about

whether I would be able to speak hopefully, especially after what I expected would be a terribly hard time at the
conference. Instead I found myself speaking with a hope-
fulness I had never known before.

> I am here today to declare that these words of hope from
> Romans 8 are true. Of course, we have all believed that, and
> we all believe it now. Yet I say today that these words are
> true in a way I have never said it before. I have for many
> years believed these words. I have sought to live on the as-
> sumption of their truth. But I have not felt, *known,* that they
> are true deep in my being. My belief has been of the "I be-
> lieve, help thou my unbelief" kind. I have clung tenaciously,
> like a bulldog, to the belief that there is hope, goodness, at
> the base of reality, even though my spirit often has not felt
> it.
>
> I was convinced, in a way, of the truth of the gospel. I
> could never free myself from its grasp. But I was also a child
> of—a victim of—the Enlightenment and the best education
> modern America can offer. Yes, I have preached and taught
> what I believed—that God is love and God calls us to love
> others, that God forgives, that God sustains the weak, that
> there is finally hope, not despair. But when I preached such
> hopeful messages in the face of the world's suffering, I wept
> inwardly—and sometimes outwardly—at the beauty and
> power of this message, and at the difficulty of feeling such
> hope at the center of my being.
>
> Mine was a "wintry faith," a tough, strong faith, a faith not
> untouched by the beauty of snowdrifted fields, but a faith
> which clings to hope for life in the way a barren tree clings
> to life as it bends before the winter wind, waiting for the
> newness of spring.
>
> I may shed tears today also, but if I do, they will be tears of
> joy. I cannot explain what happened. But I can testify that I
> know in my inmost being that these words from Romans
> are true, that I have been touched by the grace of God, that I
> sense a joy welling up which I have not known before. I am
> sure that I will not always feel the joy, the hope, the grace,

that I experience today. But I believe that I will never be able to forget the sense of springtime which I know today. When the winter winds blow again, as they shall, I will know deep inside that winter is not the only reality. Spring is not a mirage, always hoped for, always ahead, but never experienced, never touched. It is a reality, as real as winter.

As I write, winter winds are blowing again. Seven months ago Gayle and I held her father and sang "Gott ist die Liebe" ("For God So Loved Us") to him as he died in our home, his home. Five months ago our seminary president, and perhaps our closest co-worker died suddenly. Both our predictable work world and our dear friend were gone without even the possibility of a good-bye. A month ago, Gayle's mother died in our home, her home. Our day-to-day lives, our family landscape . . . strangely unfamiliar . . . an empty room. I do not always live in springtime.

Nevertheless, now I would not say that spring is as real as winter. Spring is more real. Thanks be to God!   ∎

2

A Journey Begun

Wilma Ann Bailey

"Now I lay me down to sleep. I pray the Lord my soul to keep. If I should die before I wake, I pray the Lord my soul to take." Like many other English-speaking children, I was introduced to God through this prayer.

I read somewhere that Epicurus, an Athenian philosopher who lived in the fourth century before Christ, thought that fear of the gods was the primary source of anxiety. This prayer created no anxiety for my three-year-old mind because I did not know what it meant. The concepts behind "die," "Lord," and "soul" were a mystery to me. They meant nothing.

I said the prayer because my mother told me to say it, and like most three-year-olds, I wanted to please my mom. I remember clearly the moment when I realized what I was saying. "If I should die before I wake." I could die? I could die in my sleep? That did create more than a little anxiety for me. Epicurus was right! And I said the prayer with even more fervor.

I first went to Sunday school when I was four. I remember the day. I should have gone to the nursery, but I was taken to the kindergarten room with my older sister because the Sunday school superintendent thought I would be afraid to be in a class without my sister. Me, afraid? When I was three years old and lost on a beach with that same older sister, I chose to leave her because I thought she knew a better way to find our parents—by walking along the boardwalk rather than through the crowd. I wasn't afraid of anything—when I was three. Anyway, I loved Sunday school and drank in every word.

My public school was predominantly Jewish, and the largest minority in our New York City neighborhood was Irish Catholic. Every Sunday morning, with my mom and siblings, I left our apartment on the third floor of a fourteen-story apartment building (one of seven) in our public housing project and took the subway to our Baptist church in Harlem. During the summer I went to vacation Bible school at the local Lutheran church.

The religious pluralism in which I lived told me that something was wrong with my religion. The Jewish children missed school on Jewish holidays. The Catholic children had Catholic holidays off. When my mother explained that our only holidays were Christmas (when everybody was off) and Easter (which fell on a Sunday), I knew I had been cheated! I resolved immediately to convert to Catholicism or some religion that had lots of holidays. In truth, it was not so much a day off school that I wanted as a holy-day, a day set apart from the mundane routine of lessons, homework, and play.

I remember asking my Jewish and Catholic friends about their religions. The Catholic kids went to catechism, and the Jewish kids went to Hebrew school. I wanted to go to the Lutheran Released Time classes, but my mom would not consent because she thought I would become theologically confused.

She did let me leave school early once a week to attend Released Time classes at the Baptist church. I went for a quarter but was quickly discouraged by the lack of interest of other students who apparently signed up just to get out of the public school and who behaved abominably for our well-meaning but untrained instructor. In truth, I was intensely interested in faith and religious observance ever since that first day in Sunday school but found few opportunities to nourish my faith outside of Sunday morning.

At age eleven, I decided I would be baptized when I was twelve because when Jesus was twelve he had gone to the temple and revealed his identity. But I did not necessarily want to be baptized in my church. I wanted to be baptized in the *right* church, one completely consistent with the teachings of Jesus. How could I know which church that was?

I decided to read about every religion, then choose the right one. I took out of the library books that described every religion and denomination. This was how I learned about the Mennonite Church. I remember thinking that the Mennonite Church was most faithful to the teachings of the New Testament, along with my own Baptist Church.

I did not, however, know of any Mennonite churches. So I decided to be baptized in my own church. I went upstairs to the adult service after my twelfth birthday and marched down the aisle alone as an expression of my desire to be baptized. My understanding was that I was being baptized as an outward symbol of what had already taken place in my heart. I had not had a dramatic conversion. I was just saying, "This is who I am." On the brink of adolescence, I vowed to not get into teenage trouble. I wanted to be perfect; I wanted to be a saint.

Forget modesty. I *was* a saint! I did not smoke. I did not drink. I did not spend money foolishly. I did not do drugs. I did not do sex. I did not curse or lie or steal. I read my Bible and prayed and went to church. And that probably did protect me from the kind of trouble many teenagers get themselves into.

I did not regret my sainthood for one moment then— but I do now sometimes. Sainthood isn't all it's cracked up to be. Sometimes I hear alcoholics say they just want to be sober, and inside I say, "Being sober isn't that great." No

one wants to hear from a saint. People are praised for re-
covering from something—alcohol, drugs, profligacy. No
one says to you when you are twenty, "Congratulations
for making it through your teenage years intact!" No one
asks you to speak in church about how perfect you are.

Popular Christianity is a strange religion. If you do
wrong, you are a sinner. If you do right, you are still a sinner. You can't win. You are and must be a sinner! You have
to say, "I was drunk!" "I was a whore!" "I was a drug ad-
dict" or at the very least you must confess to having im-
pure thoughts or skewed motivations—or else you have
committed another sin, the sin of pride! But I repented of
such blasphemous thoughts long ago. The world is too
complex for goodness to be absolute on the human level.

When I was fifteen, my sister and I spent a week at a Bible camp. A school friend had invited us. My only other
experience at an overnight camp was at Minisink, which
was sponsored by the Methodist Church. The Bible camp
was nothing like Minisink. Except for a few hours in the afternoon, the entire day was given over to worship, Bible
study, and trashing every denomination except that of the
camp.

I had never run into dogmatism and narrow-
mindedness before. It was not a characteristic of my congregation. And I rejected it immediately. At this camp for
the first time in my life I heard someone ask, "Are you
saved?" I remember a counselor coming over to us during
free time and posing that question. Our friend immediately jumped between the questioner and us and said, "Yes,
she is saved. I am saved. We are all saved. Praise the Lord!"

Satisfied, the counselor left. Our friend then counseled
us to give the same reply when anyone asked that question. She stressed that we should throw in a "praise the
Lord" or "hallelujah" for emphasis.

I thought that was the most ridiculous thing I had ever

heard. Jesus didn't ask people, "Are you saved?" Neither did Paul. It seemed to me the important thing was that you loved God. The words you used were not important.

This worldly friend introduced me to something else I had never thought about. We were singing our hearts out during a morning service: "Wash me and I shall be whiter than snow." My friend nudged me and whispered, "Want to bet?" We were black. To this day I do not sing "whiter than snow" songs.

The camp, however, was not all bad. I was most impressed by the dedication of the staff to their understanding of the Christian life. It was there that I started to read the Bible systematically.

My Baptist church did an excellent job of telling me what I should do to live the Christian life but a poor job of providing specific direction or opportunities to do what they told me I ought to be doing. I wanted to teach Sunday school when I was sixteen. I was told I was too young. I was saying with Isaiah, "Here am I, send me." And the church was saying, "We have no place for you."

During my last semester of my last year in high school, I began visiting other congregations. One was too big. That was the Riverside Church in New York, where I was directed to an elevator that took me to one of several balconies. The next was too small and lacked warmth. The third was just right. It was the Mennonite House of Friendship (now Friendship Community Church) in The Bronx. I had found it in the Bell Telephone book.

I was attracted to this congregation at first because its members possessed a theology compatible with my own. Then they embraced me in warmth and friendliness and provided me with literature about the church. And, importantly, they gave me a job to do. They invited me to lead a girl's club, then to teach Sunday school, then to start a youth group, then to serve on the church council, then to direct summer Bible school, then to lead worship, then to preach from the pulpit . . .

Thus by God's grace, I began my journey.   ■

Wilma Ann Bailey is assistant professor of Old Testament, Messiah College, Grantham, Pennsylvania. She received her education at Hunter/Lehman College, Associated Mennonite Biblical Seminary, and at Vanderbilt University, where she is completing her doctoral work. She has served the church on a variety of boards, including currently the Mennonite Board of Education and the Mennonite Central Committee. She has also fulfilled teaching, pastoral, and voluntary service assignments. Her writing and speaking has been addressed to both scholarly and lay audiences.

3

To Serve God and to Laugh

Peter J. Dyck

WHEN MY FATHER put his hand on my knee without saying a word or even looking at me, I wanted to laugh because that is where I am most ticklish, my knees. But I didn't dare laugh because we were in church. That is one of my earliest memories of worship. Not that I worshiped much. I just swung my legs back and forth, to the annoyance of my father, who tried to stop me while he concentrated on the sermon.

Many years later, after we had left Russia and settled in Saskatchewan, my father wrote about his spiritual struggle as a young man, his loneliness, his unhappiness, and how he had found peace with God in a most unexpected and marvelous way. He concluded this very personal testimony with these words: "O world, laugh and make fun of this experience, if you can. But I am not writing this for the world but for my dear children. Perhaps these imperfect words, which do not begin to describe the blessedness I felt, can one day strengthen you in your own pilgrimage."

Then, not wishing to appear dogmatic, he added, "If one or the other of you should not have this kind of experience, do not be discouraged. I am convinced that everyone must come to God in his and her own way, and God will draw near to us. The only condition is that we come honestly and in childlike faith."

I did not come to the Christian faith the way my father did, although his testimony has been a great blessing and encouragement to me. Faith came to me more by osmosis, like Timothy's, about which Paul said, "I am reminded of your sincere faith, a faith that lived first in your grandmother Lois and your mother Eunice and now, I am sure, lives in you" (2 Tim. 1:5).

Just when I stopped swinging my legs in church and started paying attention to the sermon, I don't remember. Nor do I remember when I first realized that listening to a sermon, however intently, was not the same as worshiping God. But I do remember that I was still quite young when it struck me that worship was serving God. Our worship services were always in German, both in Russia, and in the first years in Canada, and so we talked about the *Gottesdienst*, literally "God service." Not until many years later did I meet people who said they went to church to have their needs met, who shopped around for a church where they would get something out of it. I thought that was rather strange.

Just as I had never seen a toothbrush until the age of twelve when we came to Canada, so I had never been to a Sunday school. We had no Sunday schools in Russia. And when our beloved John Regier, pastor of Tiefengrund Mennonite Church at Laird, Saskatchewan, had catechetical instruction with us teenagers, I memorized the answers in the catechism the way we were supposed to. I was being prepared at the relatively late age of nineteen to be baptized and to join the church. I had not had a Pauline kind of conversion experience. That is not to say that these lessons and the baptism were "dry bones" for me; the experience was deeply moving.

However, I remember traveling with the choir of what is today Rosthern Junior College and being hosted in a Mennonite home in Alberta. Within five minutes after I entered his living room, our host asked whether I was saved. That question haunted me for a long time. Then, because I claimed to be a Christian, he asked me to tell him about my conversion experience. But I couldn't. That too bothered me. Later Uncle John, as we lovingly called our pastor, said he would ask me the same question, only phrase it a little differently.

"Tell me, Peter," he began, "are you walking with the Lord or not?" I unhesitatingly answered that I was walking with him, however imperfectly. With a warm smile and his hand on my shoulder, Uncle John said, "Keep going! As long as your face is toward God and not your back, don't worry."

That was more than fifty years ago and, praise God's name, I have not turned my back on him. Perhaps I should say God has not let me turn my back. I know God is drawing me to himself, that he loves me, that he has forgiven all the foolishness I've done, and that he isn't as upset as I was back in Alberta when I couldn't say exactly when or how this walking together had begun. My father walked with God and so did my grandfather, not to mention my wonderful mother and grandmother, and I walk with God too, because I don't want to walk with any other god. And I certainly don't want to walk alone!

Today my legs are too long to swing from a church bench, but I still go to church and still believe that the primary objective of worship is to serve God—Worship *is* Gottesdienst. I love to meet with the people of God, to sing the hymns of the church, to hear the same good news, which one hymn writer has called "the old, old story," over and over again, "because I know it's true; it satisfies my longing as nothing else could do."

If the man in Alberta would ask me today to tell him about my conversion experience, I would probably ask him which one because I've been converted so often.

Some of these experiences were happy and soothing, like gentle rain quenching thirsty soil, and some were extremely painful, like Paul's encounter with God on the Damascus road. But whether pleasant or painful, each experience brought me closer to the Lord and made me more aware of the fact that he has been the actor in the drama of my life, not I.

As Francis Thompson says so well in his famous poem, "The Hound of Heaven," God pursued me, blocked my way, changed my direction, guided me, encouraged me! I am sure it was God who put the longing for salvation into my heart in the first place.

Closely related to my spiritual pilgrimage, but not to be completely identified with it, is the road that led me to a total rejection of war and violence. I suppose that was inevitable because love was at the heart of both my developing spirituality and my growing peace conviction.

I do not recall in my childhood or youth ever having heard what I would call a peace sermon. Nor did I read peace books. Although we lived in the country of Leo Tolstoy, I had never read his *War and Peace*, and hadn't even heard his delightful story "Where Love Is, There God Is Also."

But I had heard my father talk about his stint in alternative service in the forests of Russia, along with twelve thousand other Mennonite men, during World War I. As a boy I picked up all kinds of bits and pieces about it—how much better it was to take a spade and plant trees than to take a gun and cut down people; how good the camp discipline was for most of the young men; how sacrificial the church was when it paid for all of this for four years; how sad it was that after the war some of these same fellows took up arms to defend themselves against the opportunist Nestor Machno; how the peace conviction had to be very personal, a matter of the heart, and not legislated from above either by church or government.

That had been the problem with some who attempted to fight off the rascal Machno when he came to plunder, burn, and rape in the Mennonite villages. They had done their four years of alternative service rather than being in the military, but the way of peace in all human relations had never been a deep personal conviction for them. They had not seen themselves as obedient disciples following their Lord so much as simply doing what was expedient and expected of them.

Years later, during World War II, these memories stood me in good stead. I was a volunteer serving with Mennonite Central Committee (MCC) in England when the draft caught up with me. The year was 1944. I was busy evacuating women, children, and old people from the burning cities to the safety of the countryside when I received the call to report for military service.

What was I do to? I enjoyed what I was doing, and I thought the army could do nicely without me. More than that, I was suddenly and unexpectedly confronted with the question of allegiance: God or country? Who was first in my life? Whom would I obey? The country said, "Kill." God said, "Love." For me, a young man in my mid-twenties, the dilemma was very real.

Oh, how I wished for counsel from my church, from my dear Uncle Regier in Tiefengrund. But the church and my own family were thousands of miles away. There were only four other Mennonites, the MCC workers, in England; they were scattered in different parts of the country. It didn't help that I knew a fifth young Mennonite stationed in England, not with MCC but the Canadian army.

I filed for release from military service on grounds of conscience and soon found myself inside a courtroom facing a judge with a wig on his head. Just as I wanted to laugh in church when my father put his hand on my knee but didn't, so now I wanted to laugh because I thought it was so funny to see a grown man looking ever so serious and having that mop on his head. Of course, I didn't laugh, but I did pray, "Lord, help me!"

The trial or hearing didn't go the way I wanted it to go so I appealed the decision. At the higher court in Manchester, Judge Burgis presided. The prosecutor worked me over, always asking the what-would-you-do-if kinds of questions. At one point in the long hearing, I turned respectfully to the judge and announced, "Your Honor, the war is over!" Of course, World War II was not over, and I had to explain that I meant that for *me* this war and any other war was over. I would not kill and destroy.

In later years I have often looked back on that moment and incident as a special moment of grace and significance in my spiritual pilgrimage. Not that I had been violent before and then declared my peaceful intention, but rather that I articulated for the first time, and in public, that I renounced all violence and would follow Jesus in the way of peace. That was good for me.

That is also how it was with my initial commitment to Christ. I don't think the man in Alberta understood that, and I was too young to explain it. But while I could not remember having had a Damascus road experience and therefore could not tell the dear brother either the date or time when I had been "saved," I do know today that it was a day of grace and tremendous importance for me when I stood before my congregation on the day of baptism and acknowledged publicly that I had accepted Jesus Christ as my Savior and Lord. In both instances what had happened by osmosis, if that is the way to describe it, became focused and demanded a conscious decision. That the decision was articulated in public was, I believe, extremely important for my further spiritual growth.

I do not regret either of these public declarations. It

was good for my further development of the peace position to have told Judge Burgis that the war was over, but
today I know that day was something like the beginning.
To be a peacemaker, as Jesus asks us to be, requires a great
deal more than saying no to violence and war. Today government doesn't want my warm body; it wants my cold
cash, and so we hassle with the Internal Revenue Service.
The struggle continues. I know that it will continue, on this
and other levels of spirituality, until I reach the end of my
road. And it is good this way.

At age eighty I think sometimes how it will be when
this life is over, and I'll sit on a cloud riding into the next
world. Knowing myself I think I'll probably just want to sit
there, swing my legs, and laugh. Not the laugh of a boy because somebody tickles his knees, and not the laugh because something is funny, like a wig on a man's head—but
the laugh of a child who is delighted and happy because
his Father has made all things well.

Soli Deo gloria!   ■

Peter Dyck was born into the chaos of war, revolution, and
famine in Russia. In 1927, at age twelve, he migrated to
Canada with his family. Since 1941 Peter has given most of
his energies to Mennonite Central Committee, working in
and directing MCC programs in Europe, resettling refugees, and telling the story of God's work through MCC.
He has also served as a pastor. In more recent years, he has
written several books of children's fiction. *Up from the
Rubble* (Herald Press, 1991) is an autobiographical account
by Peter and his wife, Elfrieda, about their work with MCC
in Europe during and after World War II. They have two
daughters and five grandchildren.

4

Contending Against Wrong Without Being Wrongly Contentious

Marian Franz

DURING TWELVE YEARS of living in a poor and overcrowded Chicago ghetto while my husband, Delton, pastored the Woodlawn Mennonite Church, we were close to the families of four two-year-old children who died needlessly. One died because of faulty wiring, one was bitten by a rat, one was in an apartment fire, and the fourth was poisoned by lead paint that had fallen into his crib. My rural Kansas Mennonite upbringing had taught me what to do when people die. You visit their families with Scripture and potato salad. These tragic, needless deaths occurred so rapidly, however, that I could never make enough potato salad.

The call of Christ was, "Stop the dying." To do that, we looked at city codes which allowed wealthy landlords to collect exorbitant rents without making apartments safe. The touch of Christ was not on the drawing board when those laws were made. I knew then that it *is* the Christian's duty to go to government to tend "the least of these."

So when the call came in the late 1960s to Delton and me to go to Washington, D.C., and open the Mennonite Central Committee office there, we went. One evening soon after we arrived, we attended a dinner at the Church of the Saviour, a downtown Washington church. My Mennonite instincts were still quite intact. At the dinner table, I introduced myself to the person sitting beside me. "Hello, I'm Marian Franz."

"Hello, I'm Bill Price."

"What do you do, Bill?" I asked.

"I'm the highest ranking civilian at the Pentagon," he explained. "I'm director of the United States Air Force Office of Scientific Research, which works on laser beam weaponry for the air force."

I drew back in shock. Emitting a loud gasp, I blurted, "How *could* you?"

My astonishment astonished Bill. He was used to quite a different response to questions about his career. Usually people were impressed with his high position, showed due deference, and offered laudatory comments. He was curious about my offense and astonishment.

"Those weapons kill *people!*" I said, still sputtering my simple and horrified response.

Bill courteously explained he was proud he had brought a new system of management to his department at the Pentagon. As a result, the department was running more efficiently.

"Having an office work efficiently is generally commendable," I said, then persisted in refocusing the conversation on the victims of such efficiency. "How can you be involved in taking the lives of others in such a calculating manner? Those are *real* people—parents, babies, teenagers, the elderly, God's children—at the other end of those weapons."

Within a year Bill Price resigned his position and left the Pentagon. With others at the Church of the Saviour, he and his wife, Betty, founded World Peacemakers, an organization he has headed for many years.

I never forgot the incident at the dinner table—that

gasp and my initial chill and shock. Feeling a little embarrassed by my behavior, I half-hoped Bill had forgotten our conversation.

Years later I learned that a group of students who interviewed Bill about World Peacemakers asked, "We know you used to work at the Pentagon. Why did you quit?"

"Let me tell you what contributed to my change," Bill said. "One evening in the late '60s, I was having dinner at my church. There was a lady sitting beside me . . ."

After more than twenty-five years in the nation's capital, I have long since lost that original sense of shock when people calmly defend their military activities. Yet for the sake of the victims of military violence, should I not remain scandalized?

The ancient prophets never became accustomed to wrong. They were not callous to their own callousness. They felt a supreme impatience and indignation with evil. Their outrage was expressed in superlatives: "Be shocked! Be utterly desolate! Be appalled, O heavens, at this!" By comparison, might we not be guilty of indecent composure?

I cannot think of anything more precious, more promising, or more demanding than Jesus' call to tend "the least of these." That obligation includes "speaking truth to power" (a classic Quaker phrase). Such witness means far more than covering things up with a smile or holding those in power at a distance with politeness, however.

Because peace advocates and military generals live in separate worlds, the peace movement sees the military establishment as a collection of misguided people, protected by bureaucratic formality from all contact with reality. The military establishment perceives the peace movement as a collection of naive people, meddling in a business they do not understand. Each group considers itself right. Each considers itself morally superior.

The two sides remain polarized because each usually preaches only to its own. Too often when conversation is attempted, it succeeds only in creating more barriers to understanding. But all our theologies of church and state, of religious freedom and governance, of divine law and human law, are in the end transmitted in rather ordinary person-to-person encounters. After hundreds of visits to members of the Senate and House of Representatives, I can tell you something. I have never met "the Congress." I have never engaged in a dialogue with "the state" or conversed with a policy. I *do* meet people—just plain people.

Unless I accept the spirit of nonviolence and speak the truth in love, I can wage my own form of war between "us" and "them." If pride, anger, or cynicism creep in, we become agitators rather than peacemakers. We wage a new battle of words to gain our own kind of "victory." When the impatient among us write politicians off as "nothing but political animals," we cut ourselves off from the beauty and power of loving human encounter and creative witness. Our conversation is, after all, not a confrontation between evil and innocence. Only in an atmosphere of trust can we discuss hard issues.

"My mind was changed on arms funding," said one member of Congress, "by persons who did not polarize the debate into 'us' and 'them.' These people helped transform my attitude because they helped me see the facts and decide for myself without making me their enemy."

I have found it easy to make scapegoats of the military and proponents of the military. Blaming, however, closes listening ears and triggers the need to strike back. If I take an exalted, self-righteous stance and point an accusing finger, I mimic the game of blame played out by warring countries. Each of them pursues self-justification by decrying the parallel sins of the other side. Only those without sin are allowed to cast stones.

If we aim stones, we miss the opportunity to learn important lessons about ourselves. Especially we miss seeing our own culpability. If blame is to be assessed, we might examine our own share by looking at ourselves, our peace organizations, our religious bodies, our souls. Jesus calls us to examine our own moral sieves which, without tending, can become so distorted that they strain out gnats, but not camels.

The challenge for us is to stop assessing blame and start assuming responsibility. When the disciples learned their Lord was to be betrayed, they did not blame. Each asked, "Is it I?"

Like any cross section of citizens, men and women with political power make decisions from a variety of motives. I have seen many try hard, struggle against great odds, and make decisions at the risk of their own political careers. Considerations such as job security, political welfare, economics, and feasibility often enter the formal decision-making process. Deliberations on moral and ethical aspects of these decisions, however, take place deep within the legislators themselves, sometimes in loneliness, sometimes with a few trusted individuals.

When I raise issues, I am aware I may magnify the internal pressures of those in power. In some instances it is painful to watch as many struggle to accommodate both the religious and the political dimensions of their own experience. These conflicts are experienced in acute form. The struggles are not simply intellectual. They touch the deepest springs of personal feeling. Policymakers bear these conflicts at great physical and psychological cost. Legislators need us to continually raise issues, but at the same time they need us to respect them as precious, unique, and worth our continued support and attention *no matter what their decisions.*

We will help them most when we do good things in a

good way; when we counter national self-righteousness without personal self-righteousness; when we contend against wrong without being wrongly contentious.

Policymakers are confronted by many people trying to get their attention and persuade them to make certain decisions. Among the persuaders or lobbyists in the U.S. Capitol are those some call "hired guns." They are highly paid lobbyists for large corporations and wealthy interest groups. Their suasion stems not from moral commitment to their cause. Everyone knows they are paid to speak the company line and could just as easily lobby for a different organization for another paycheck. These hired guns are listened to because they have the means to offer rewards and punishments, lollipops and spankings, depending on whether or not the member of Congress toes their line.

Once, in the reception room of a congressional office, I was surrounded by lobbyists in military uniforms and hired guns in expensive suits. To me, those in military uniforms and silk suits represented the military-industrial complex in microcosm. In the company of such overwhelming power, I felt intimidated and diminished, as I felt when the congressman's aide invited me into the office with a "How are you?"

"I feel like I am being squeezed between the military and the industrial, and it is giving *me* a complex," I replied.

His response was notable. "Many groups like yours carry an entirely different persuasive power," he said, "because it is based on a conviction about right and wrong, about the morality or immorality of a given policy."

He continued, "If the group is composed of *true believers* deeply committed to their cause, that intensity of feeling can multiply the group's influence far beyond its numbers."

True belief, a movement of conscience whose cry for justice and peace is rooted in the Bible rather than political ideology, is the hardest to discredit or ignore. True belief, by definition, entails principles that will not yield. Refusal to yield results in sacrifice. Anyone who believes deeply is a potential martyr. That is the measure and the nature of belief. Others cannot understand that belief unless we express it clearly by faithful words and faithful actions.

We do not claim to be experts in every field, but we can proclaim our own expertise on conscience and speak to the moral and ethical dimensions of congressional issues. We must do so with humility, recognizing the possible limitations of our own vision. "To confess the sins of another," a theologian has said, "is not a religious act." Martin Luther exemplified this. His moral power came not by saying . . . "Here is where you should stand"; rather, Luther said, "Here I stand; I can do no other."

True prophets do not ignore their inward life or lose a sense of their sacred image. They know the stillness of a commitment that sustains them in the long, difficult run. Prophets listen to God and others. Prophets feel fiercely because they hear deeply. They pray for those to whom they prophesy.

Sometimes the Lord's Prayer becomes my prayer of intercession. In place of "Our Father," we can pray, "Senator John Doe's father" (using the senator's first name). When he comes to "Thy kingdom come," we can say, "May the kingdom come to John. . . . Give John this day daily bread. . . . Lead John not into temptation." Then we might list in our prayer the myriad temptations John faces to put political position over human need, to care more for the rich than for the poor. Hymns also make good intercessory prayers.

When I invest the time to care deeply for individuals in honest, substantive, prayerful relationships, I find I see legislators differently. In a world where lobbyists want only to get the legislator on one side of an issue or another, then leave after a "hit and run" approach, people in power experience a unique loneliness.

Sometimes, just when I wonder whether the investment of my time and witness really makes a difference, I become aware of a hunger. A congresswoman with whom I became friends despite the fact we sometimes disagreed wrote, "Dear Mrs. Franz, . . . The Christian love you have shown me means more than I will ever be able to express. . . . Perhaps you have found . . . a type of political involvement which, over the long run, will make more of a difference than any other kind. . . . Many members of Congress, if they could have a relationship like this, would cherish that relationship more than any other. At least I do."

I know now that the same love which binds me to the victims of oppression and war binds me also to the powerful. I know that unless the gospel is alive in a people, little hope exists that it will take root and flourish on the crowded path of public life. When a member of Congress says, "The way you go about your work, so quietly, and wanting nothing for yourselves, is the single most powerful thing I have seen on Capitol Hill," I know God takes our small gifts and makes them beautiful. To have that gift received by God is the greatest satisfaction I know.   ∎

Marian Claassen Franz is executive director of the National Campaign for a peace Tax Fund and of the Peace Tax Foundation in Washington. In pursuit of peace tax legislation, she interprets to Congress the conscience-driven values of persons who assert their right not to participate in killing other human beings through their military taxes. Educated at Bethel (Kansas) College and Mennonite Biblical Seminary (then in Chicago), she has been active in a wide variety of church speaking and committee assignments for many years. Currently she is a member of the General Board of the General Conference Mennonite Church.

5

Converting the Preacher: Unlikely Evangelists

Paul M. Gingrich

"OH, MR. GINGRICH," he said, "I don't mind if you get angry with me. That's the way all of the big white Americans are. You do not need to apologize."

Zewdie ("my throne") had just delivered another armload of wood to our kitchen. As had happened many times before, Zewdie had cut the wood too long—too long for our imported wood-burning stove. When the wood was too long, the stove plates would not shut completely. Smoke billowed from the top of the stove rather than going up the chimney.

I was angry. This was not the first time I had told Zewdie, in my most polite, patient voice, to "cut the wood shorter, please." I had even made him a nice gauge so he could check the length. But this time I had exploded at him, full of superior, Western indignation. I used words which reflected unfavorably on his parentage, intellectual ability, aptitude, general character, age, and even stature. (He was a short, old man.)

How could he be so dumb? He had only one job, cutting wood. He had just one specification—providing the right length—and he couldn't even manage that. What should I do? Fire him on the spot? Reduce his seventy-five cents-a-day wage? I stormed into the house. I would force him to cut the wood right!

I went back to my study to prepare a lesson for the Bible class which would meet in one hour. I sat at my desk with an open Bible and a prayerful attitude, but the image of Zewdie kept popping into my mind. The more I tried to forget the sound of my angry voice, the louder it became.

I was twenty-five and a new missionary in Ethiopia. I had been given the post of chief executive officer in a hospital operated for the government by the mission. I didn't know much of the local language, and I was frustrated by the ineptness of the Ethiopian "servants." They moved slowly. They stopped to talk. They took time for tea and siesta. How were we to operate an efficient hospital with people like these? The burden of this anger caused me to be depressed and unhappy, though I tried to be a nice missionary. I wanted so badly to succeed.

But my angry outbursts happened frequently. I had physical pains. I was sick in bed often and at the point of saying, "Let's go back to America where everything is right, and people know how to do things."

As I sat at my desk, an inner voice said, "You must go to Zewdie and apologize for your offensive behavior."

"Who, me?" I asked. "I should apologize to Zewdie? For what?"

"For absolutely inappropriate behavior against an innocent person," the voice said.

"Stop thinking those dumb thoughts," I said to myself. "This little guy is just a woodcutter. Should I, chief of hospital administration, director of the school, pastor of the congregation, apologize to Zewdie, this nobody?"

My inner voice said, "Yes, that's what you must do."

My stomach contracted. Spasms of fear gripped me. How could I lower myself to apologize to this preliterate, simple woodcutter? How would this appear to the other workers? Would I lose respect and soon have all the servants "cutting the wood too long"? As I hesitated and rationalized, I knew deep down that an apology would be right, but I dallied. Here I was the person with status, responsibility, prestige, power. In every other situation of confession and restitution, I had dealt with someone of equal or higher status. I had never needed to ask forgiveness of a lowly servant.

I continued to argue with myself. The Bible class came and went. I taught something, but my heart wasn't in it. The battle raging in my soul would not be stilled. This was a broken relationship. How could I make this wrong right without the pain of a face-to-face apology? I tried desperately to imagine other ways to resolve my self-made conflict. None worked. As soon as I'd rationalize away the wrongness of my behavior, a new wave of guilt would come over me.

Finally after hours of struggle, I decided to go to Zewdie and apologize. I found Zewdie still chopping wood.

He greeted me with a warm smile and said, "Hello, Master (*Getoch*)."

I stumbled around in Amharic and finally said, "I'm really sorry for getting angry at you, Zewdie. That was wrong. I have sinned. Will you forgive me?"

Zewdie looked at me with understanding eyes. And in his eyes I could sense the wisdom of Africa, the ability to know the truth without having it explained.

Zewdie answered, "Oh, Mr. Gingrich, I don't mind if you get angry with me. That's the way all of the big white Americans are. You do not need to apologize."

The inference caused me to cringe—"After all, you *are* the *Master*."

Beside that woodpile, I heard the voice of God in poor, old, nonbelieving Zewdie's words. God said, "Paul, if you are going to succeed in this land, you must be converted. I do not need your Western, superior, overpowering, and self-important ministry. I need people who know how to

repent and who will work with Ethiopians as servant partners. There is only one Master. You will serve me best
when you humble yourself. Forget your education, culture, and feelings of superiority. Let me teach you a new
way."

At first I did not name my angry outbursts as prejudice.
I thought this was just the way I was. So there were many
other events similar to my encounter with Zewdie at the
woodpile—so many, in fact, that the Ethiopians with
whom I worked began to give me uncomplimentary nick-
names like "The Hot Head" and "Bald One."

One of my best teachers was Negussie ("my king"), another Ethiopian who came to work with me in the nurse's
aide training school. Negussie was an energetic, quick-
learning leader. He had relatives who were close to the
king, Haile Selassie I, and he was the opposite of Zewdie.
In Negussie, I met my match. When I got angry or expressed frustration with Ethiopians, he would stand toe-
to-toe with me and return my angry outburst with the
same force. He interpreted my anger for what it was: racism. I began to learn slowly and painfully that conversion
is a long process, and that a quick apology or request for
forgiveness cannot be an excuse for continued sinning.

Little by little I learned to recognize the real cause for
my angry outbursts. With the help of patient Ethiopians, I
came to confess my feelings of superiority. I had come to
Africa to help convert, teach, and lead. This was naive ig-
norance. I had come to give, and when this gift—myself—
was not received with deep gratitude and submissive
thanks, I reacted in anger. I thought, *How could these people
resist my gift when I made such great sacrifices to come to them
as a missionary?*

My culturally narrow ideas that Western church and
Western culture were superior needed to be converted.
These views began to change as I learned to receive—first

from Zewdie, then from Negussie, and later from many, many others. When I could receive their counsel, ideas, visions and criticism, I could also receive their forgiveness. Mutual forgiveness grew into mutual respect. This respect for Ethiopians helped me step out of the way so they could become educated and hold leadership positions. When Ethiopians took over leadership responsibilities once carried by Western expatriates, the church became truly Ethiopian.

It is now more than forty years since those early days in Ethiopia. I can still see Zewdie—ax in hand with a loving, innocent smile on his face. That day God started to cleanse me of my racial prejudice. That day I saw with new eyes that Africans had something to give *me*. ■

Paul and Ann Gingrich went to Ethiopia in 1954 and returned to the United States in 1969. After ten years at Goshen (Indiana) College working in church relations and campus ministry, Paul became president of Mennonite Board of Missions in 1980. Strong ties have been maintained with the growing Ethiopian church and many deep friendships made during residence in Ethiopia continue. Five of the six Gingrich children were born in Africa. They also love the land and its people.

6

The Dream

Ursula Lundall Green

I HAVE ALWAYS been a dreamer. No, I don't mean a day-dreamer or a visionary. I just mean that I dream when I sleep and often remember my dreams when I awake.

Sometimes the dreams are about ordinary everyday things. Sometimes they're confused and crazy. Sometimes they recall people and places long forgotten by my conscious mind. Sometimes they're scary and leave me feeling shaken. One dream I'll not forget as long as I live, for it has impacted my life forever.

It was a simple dream. I don't recall any words being said, but the image disturbed me. Let me take you back to February 4, 1975, the day I had the dream.

I awoke from my unsettling dream with a start, hearing the matron of our hostel call my name. For a few dazed moments, I didn't know where I was. Soon I realized she was calling me to the phone. Throwing on my robe and flip-flops, I ran to the lobby, where the only phone serving some fifty young women stood.

"Wake up, sleepyhead!" It was my mom's cheery voice. She'd just called to say hello and that she missed and loved me.

It was Tuesday of the second week of the new school year, my third year at Bechet Teacher Training College in Durban, South Africa. Since the first week had started on Wednesday, I hadn't gone home for the weekend as usual.

After a rushed shower I grabbed my school bag and

brown-bag lunch and ran the ten minutes to school. I hated to be late. Out of breath, I collapsed into my desk. Our teacher was not yet in the classroom. My classmates were working quietly on some assignments.

Finally I had a moment to reflect on my dream. *Daddy was crying on my shoulder as he hugged me close.* That was all I could remember. I felt a moment of dread.

Toward the end of the day, our teacher shared with us the exciting news that the music department was going to present the musical *Carmen Jones*, by Oscar Hammerstein II (based on *Carmen*, by Bizet). We left college that afternoon with a sense of excited anticipation. We would audition and then memorize lines and songs. It was going to be a great year!

While I walked to the hostel alone, my feelings of dread returned. The simple image of Dad's sobs reverberated in my memory.

Daddy and Mommy had been protective and loving as we grew up. There was no doubt that they loved Lester, Evan, and me. They made every sacrifice to ensure us as comfortable and happy a childhood as they could provide.

Mom was the sunshine of our home. Her laughter and understanding of my teenage problems made me the envy of some of my girlfriends. Dad worked hard as a sheet metal worker in the day. Nights and weekends he spent preparing Bible studies and sermons, visiting the sick, and carrying out all the endless tasks of a pastor. Like me, he showed his emotions without shame. Ours was by no means a perfect family, but we knew we were loved.

The gong summoned us to dinner. As usual the hostel dining room buzzed with the chatter and laughter of young women sharing their day's experiences. Soon after dinner, the matron called me to the phone. Twice in one day wasn't bad for me.

This time the caller was Ruth, an old family friend.

Ruth was maybe eight years my senior. My family had known Ruth's family from way before any of us children were born. When I had grade eight at a school in Durban, Ruth's parents had been entrusted with my care. So I knew Ruth well.

"Ursh, my parents are going to 'Maritzburg in about a half hour. They will pick you up, so be ready, okay? Bye." She said good-bye before I could ask any questions.

My mind was reeling as I rose from the phone seat. What should I do first? I had a terrible knot in my stomach. As calmly as I could, I went upstairs to ask my friends to pray for me. I was going home in the middle of the week and didn't know why. I went to my room to pack a few clothes. I was ready when they pulled up. Or was I? We exchanged somber greetings and were soon on the familiar highway home.

A stifling silence, broken only by Aunty Francis' occasional chastising of Uncle Alfie for driving too fast, suffocated the little hope to which I was trying to cling. I didn't dare ask questions, but my mind jumped back and forth, now praying earnestly, now trusting that all was in God's care, now rehearsing all kinds of terrible scenarios.

The hour-long drive seemed an eternity. But finally we were on Sanderson Road, my neighborhood since I was a year old. The street was lined with cars, mostly of church people, I noticed. Our steps and veranda were filled with milling people, all familiar, all loved, all looking dazed. I opened the door before the car came to a halt and ran up those steps, by twos, to the unknown dread.

Daddy came out to meet me. "Thank you, God, he's safe," I breathed. Evan and Lester, my brothers, were next. They all silently hugged me, their eyes swollen and red.

Where's Mommy? my mind begged! *She must be consoling someone. Granny must be sick or maybe even dead. . . . Where's Mommy?* My eyes searched longingly, desperately among the many sad eyes that lined our long hallway. Daddy gently led us into his and Mommy's bedroom, away from those sad and curious eyes.

"Urshie, it's Mommy . . . an accident!" He hugged me close and cried on my shoulder.

* * *

Our family circle was broken that night. Daddy had us hold each other, leaving a gap between him and Lester. He cried out to God to stay near us and to help us be witnesses of grace. We walked out of the bedroom into the caring embrace of our family. All the church family, and sisters and brothers from other churches, enveloped us with their kindness.

It took me more than fifteen minutes to walk from the bedroom to our living room. The long hallway was lined with familiar faces, love and compassion exuding from their eyes unashamedly. How I needed those warm embraces! We hugged and listened to encouraging words, ate meals prepared with love, heard stories of how much Mom had meant in the lives of many individuals.

That night, when everybody went home, Daddy told us of the love he had lost, of the support and encouragement without which he didn't think he could live. My dream came back to me. Daddy needed me to be strong for him. I determined that, with God's help, I would be.

The beautiful summer sunlight streaming into my cool blue room awakened me. I lay quietly for a while feeling disturbed by the terrible dream I had just had. I had dreamed that Mommy had been killed in a car accident. The terrible ache I felt in my chest was so real.

As sleep gave way to alertness, I realized it had not been a dream. It was true! That was why I was in my own room and not at college. I didn't feel like getting up to face the day. Then I remembered my determination to be a support to Daddy. All my life my dad had given of himself unselfishly; this was my opportunity to give back. I had also decided that the vital ministry that Mom had had was my responsibility. I asked God to give me a portion of my mother's joyful spirit, kindness, and love for others.

The next day we went shopping for clothes for the funeral. As we stood at a stoplight, waiting for it to change, I noticed that everyone seemed oblivious to the significance of the day. Everyone went about their own business. Friends were giggling across the street . . . a little child was fussing, and his mother looked frustrated . . . workmen on a scaffold went on with their painting . . . a car driver honked impatiently . . . the flower vendor was calling the passersby to consider his wares. . . .

How can you all go on as though nothing has happened? I screamed in silent protest.

We got through those days by God's grace and the sheer energy we derived from all of the love poured out upon us. I remember feeling carried by God. My faith never felt stronger. Heaven never seemed closer.

My own private little joke those days after my mom's death kept me smiling. I imagined that God had a sense of humor and, just to try Mom's patience, had assigned her to harp-shining duty for a thousand years. I knew how much that would frustrate her. She would much rather be in the Celestial Choir in the Throne Room—how she loved to sing!—or simply basking in the glory of Jesus as she sat at his feet. Or perhaps she would want to arrange a party for the cherubs. Or be out fellowshipping with saints from all the ages, asking her questions of Moses, Isaiah, or Paul.

"Have patience, Mommy, you have plenty of time for all of that!" I communicated to her somewhere out there.

* * *

During those days I experienced the lavishness of God's love in a personal and tangible way. In addition, a young seminary student who visited to sympathize with our family found a lasting place for himself in our family and in my heart. In a strange way it seemed that for me life couldn't have been better.

But the euphoria of feeling connected to the very God of the universe faded with time. I've heard it said that time heals. For me, dream turned into nightmare in the months and years that followed, as I grappled with the loss of my first and best friend.

The circumstances surrounding her death made it harder. After her motor accident, the ambulance took her to the hospital for our race group, but the operating room was not equipped to handle her very serious injuries.

They then took her to the "Whites Only" hospital across town. While the paramedics were trying to reach someone who could grant permission to have her battered, bleeding body contaminate their white, sterile operating room, my precious mother died alone.

The pain I experienced didn't reconcile with the words the preacher had said at her funeral. I felt, though, that I had consciously chosen the way I was going to respond to my mother's death. When the depression and horrendous nightmares haunted me, I covered those negatives as best I could, and I existed. A dark night of despair descended, dimming the dreams I had for service.

I had begun to think God could have no use for me, one who no longer experienced abundant life, whose prayers seemed only to ricochet and never penetrate the darkness. Joy had become an illusory ray occasionally peaking from behind that ever present cloud of despair.

Years later, an encounter with a sister who had emerged from the darkness of depression to effective ministry restored my hope. When she told her story with honesty and vulnerability, I realized that what I was experiencing was not necessarily a problem of spirituality. Though I served in leadership roles for the local and larger church throughout much of two bouts of severe depression and the low-grade depression that darkened every day, I felt I was living a lie.

New hope, born out of the encounter with this sister, allowed me to see that grief not acknowledged and worked through, coupled with chemical changes in my body, contributed to my darkness. Those problems could be addressed. Again the dream of being a herald of hope, as Mom had been, was awakened in me.

God has blessed me with a wonderful husband who stood by me, with love, through the darkness; two sons who fill our home with joy; and gracious friends who listen with the heart. But there will always be an empty Mom-shaped place in my heart! She taught me how to love unselfishly, laugh unreservedly, and live uncompromisingly. "That I will do, for you, Mom, and for me, and I will pursue my dream of serving Christ and, with joy, those whose hope is dim. 'Till I see you in the morning!" ∎

Ursula Green was born and grew up in South Africa. She trained as an elementary school teacher and taught school at various levels. She married Stanley W. Green in 1977. They have a teenage son, Lee, and a preteenage son, James. The Greens spent five years in Jamaica as fraternal workers with the United Church of Jamaica and Grand Cayman. While living in Pasadena, California, the Greens became members of the Pasadena Mennonite Church. Ursula is currently upgrading her teaching credentials at Goshen (Indiana) College, where the family has lived since 1993.

7

Falling in Love with Jesus

Carolyn Holderread Heggen

As a fifth grader in a Puerto Rican mission school, I was deeply moved one day by a simple flannelgraph story of Jesus, the loving Shepherd, who searches and searches throughout a stormy night for one lost lamb. The visiting storyteller convinced me that Jesus was indeed more like a loving, tender Shepherd than the judgmental, harsh spy-in-the-sky I'd understood God to be. A tender, compassionate Jesus was someone with whom I wanted to be in relationship. So I made a heartfelt, public commitment acknowledging my desire to walk as Jesus' child.

Walking home from school that day, I had the astounding sense that I wasn't really touching the ground but was instead gliding about six inches above it, kept afloat by a wonderful, mysterious power. I decided that angels had come to give me this proof that Jesus was real and was with me in a new way since I had made a public confession of belief and commitment. I was overcome with a feeling of profound love for Jesus and for the first time thought I knew what people meant by being "in love."

Wanting to learn more about Jesus and wanting to establish good Christian habits, I committed myself to daily prayer and Bible reading. Although my parents encouraged me to start with the New Testament, I was not a child who took shortcuts or did things halfway. I began reading the Bible at the very beginning.

My Bible reading project began soon after an older,

wiser missionary kid explained to me how babies are made. As I read Genesis, the first question I wanted to discuss with someone was, "If almost everyone had only sons, how did the human race survive through those years?"

My teacher's response was more unsettling than my childish misconception. "There were probably about equal numbers of boys and girls born," she assured me. "However, few daughters get mentioned or named because they aren't important to most of the biblical stories, and there isn't enough room in the Bible to include everything and everybody."

I felt confused. Why weren't women's names and experiences considered important enough to get equal space in the biblical story? I believed God had written the Bible and was puzzled about why God would overlook half the human race in such an important document, a book with eternal life-and-death implications for all people. Nonetheless, I kept reading.

By the time I reached the book of Judges, I decided it might be important and interesting for boys and men to read the Bible, but it certainly wasn't clear to me that this book was intended for females. No girl I knew liked to read violent stories about war, attack, and conquest. The six books of the Bible I had plowed through had more violence than I'd ever been exposed to before. I decided not only that I didn't have the stomach for reading the Bible but that it took too much effort to find stories to which I could relate. Thus my childhood commitment to read through the Bible fizzled out somewhere in mid-Judges.

In junior high and high school, I again tried to develop regular habits of personal Bible study. After all, how could I keep claiming to be a Christian (and president of the local Youth for Christ club, no less) if I weren't regularly studying the Bible? New Year after New Year the resolution on the top of my list was to read the Bible regularly. But Bible reading became an increasingly frustrating experience. Where were the women's stories? Where was the female perspective? Did the Bible really have anything to do with me?

I remember well my anxiety when I first seriously thought about the story of God asking Abraham to sacrifice Isaac. What kind of God would ask a parent to kill a child? This God didn't sound any different from the blood-thirsty Aztec gods I'd been learning about in school. Furthermore, where was Isaac's mother in this story? I couldn't imagine that a mother would allow someone to kill her child, for whatever reason, without putting up a terrible fight. How could the biblical account completely ignore her?

Time after time I would reflect on a biblical story and conclude, "This doesn't make any sense to me; it doesn't fit with my feelings or experiences." Many times I felt angry and cheated that God didn't include more women's perspectives and stories in the Bible. I found that I approached the Bible feeling like an outsider, always having to work my way from outside the narrative into the story with great (and often impossible) leaps of imagination. Sometimes, if I tried hard enough, I could play a mind game and pretend that when the Bible said "men" or "son" it also meant me and my kind. But other times it seemed like just that—a mind game, a self-deceptive, futile maneuver.

As the years went by, I turned to the Bible less and less when I wanted to experience connection with God. Instead I tried to find women who passionately knew God. I read diaries and biographies of spiritual women. Increasingly I sought out women to talk to about their experiences of God. Thus began for me intentional connection with other women who were willing to share from their own inner experience of the divine.

Before going off to a church college, I was warned by several well-meaning Christian people about the likelihood that I might be exposed to heresy. Indeed, as I sat in first-semester Bible class and heard that the Bible had been written mostly by men, canonized by men, translated and interpreted by men, my first hunch was that this was the heresy about which I had been warned!

But I quickly saw the implications of such information —perhaps my sense of alienation and invisibility in relation to the Bible was not due to who God is but due to the way the Bible was written and interpreted. Perhaps my constant need to fill in the empty spaces and silences of the Bible was not a reflection of God's low regard for me. Perhaps it was a reflection of the culture in which the Bible was written and in which I live.

My newfound hope was short-lived. As I grew into adulthood and developed stronger ties with my denomination, I was saddened to see how much of myself I had to suppress to fit gracefully into the church. Much of the language about God and God's family violated my sense of the divine and God's longing to be inclusive. Having made a shaky peace with the exclusive biblical language and perspective, I increasingly became sensitive to ways the church holds up masculinity as more reflective of God's image than femininity.

As I considered career choices, I was consciously aware that there were certain gifts and interests I had which would be more welcomed in the church were I male. I thought of the preachers, the leaders, the institutional presidents and theologians who led my denomination. They were all men. This deeply saddened me.

Had I been male, I would have studied to be a preacher. Instead I became a teacher, then a psychotherapist. I became increasingly interested in the relationship between mental health and religious beliefs. I was moved by the large number of Christian women I knew who struggled with deep feelings of worthlessness. Many voiced the belief that as women they (thanks to Eve's nasty role in the Fall) were less capable of making valid moral judgments and decisions than men.

Many women truly believed that God passes out spiritual gifts based on gender considerations. Many truly felt they could trust their husbands to be the voice of God for them whether or not those men were spiritually mature persons. As I listened to women and did research with clergy, I became aware that there are popular religious teachings about women and men which set up women for depression and feelings of worthlessness.

One of my deeply held beliefs is that any teaching which isn't good news for all people, including the most vulnerable among us, is a distortion of Jesus' gospel. Said another way, I believe that true religious beliefs will positively affect mental health. Wanting to test this, I welcomed the opportunity some years ago in graduate school to do research on this topic.

I began an intense year-long process of interviewing over three hundred women. I administered tests on their religious beliefs and mental health. I reviewed the literature on the role of women in Christianity from our early Judaic roots up through women's role in the new Christian right.

The results of this investigation were personally devastating, both spiritually and emotionally. My anxiety increased as I listened to women tell stories of how religious teachings had been used to keep them in their place and to convince them that they couldn't trust themselves to know God's will without the help of a man.

As I analyzed the research data, I saw a strong relationship between feelings of worthlessness and women's belief that God intended women to live in unilateral submission to men. I wept to think of the psychological and spiritual damage being done to my Christian sisters around the world. As I read the literature on the role of women and religious attitudes toward them in early Judaism and early Christianity, in the Patristic Age and the Middle Ages, during the Reformation, and in modernity, I cringed to think that this was my people's story.

This project triggered a profound crisis of faith for me. In addition to the burden of these historical readings, I saw the contemporary and almost monthly reports of abuse by some of my denomination's best-known leaders. For years I had dared believe that my personal experiences were flukes. Increasingly I was forced to acknowledge that my violation was not just my own but in fact reflected the experience of thousands and thousands of other women and children in Christian homes and churches.

How could I identify with Christianity when it was increasingly apparent that some Christian teachings and practices were directly related to injustice and violence against women and children? What did the God I had met in experiences of transcendence and in godly women's lives have to do with any of this?

Perhaps I had been right, as a little girl first attempting to read the Bible, when I concluded that the Bible didn't have much to do with me. Perhaps I had been wrong as a young adult to struggle so hard to translate male-centered Christianity into language and metaphors which were somewhat compatible with my female experience. Perhaps it was time finally to throw out not just the bathwater but the baby too. Maybe it was time to stop pretending I conscientiously could be a Christian if I just kept struggling to transform sexist Christian images, to reinterpret the exclusive language, to fill in the painful silences about me and my sisters.

In the midst of my anguish, I had the opportunity to visit India twice. I had previously lived in Pakistan and had witnessed the oppression of women in much Islamic teaching and practice. But didn't Hinduism, among its thousands of gods, offer some female deities with whom women might identify? Wasn't this perhaps an improvement for women over Christianity with its predominantly male conceptualization of the divine?

Ironically, I found that even in Hinduism with its smorgasbord of female and male deities, the important Laws of Manu insist that a woman must worship her husband as a god, even though he may be cruel and virtueless. Anyone assessing the plight of women in India would have to conclude that having a choice of female and male deities has not been enough to make life easy or just for Indian women.

While visiting a self-help project run by Catholic nuns for some of India's most down-and-out women, I spoke with one of the sisters about despair and hope. I asked where she found the motivation to keep working in the midst of such overwhelming odds.

She told me, "When I read about Jesus, I know he'd be right down here working alongside these destitute women, and that makes me want to be here too!"

I determined that when I returned home I would re-read the gospel stories of Jesus. Thus began an experience with the Bible unlike any I had had. I told God I was touchy about the book—about the way it had been written, about the way I felt invisible in most of the stories, about the way it had been used in church and society to exclude women and keep them subjected to male control. I told God I was angry that any potentially important message in the Bible hadn't been kept a little less corrupted by cultural distortions and offensive language and metaphors. I also told God that I was desperate and committed to rereading the Gospels one more time to see if there was any word of hope for me.

And so I began reading Matthew. I gritted my teeth and plowed through the forty-some men's names (with a couple women's names thrown in for clarification) which make up the genealogy of Jesus. When I reached the fifth chapter, something happened to me. I realized I was crying but didn't know why.

I went back and reread the Beatitudes. I was overwhelmed with amazement and awe that a man in that culture (or any culture) would lift up the poor in spirit, those who mourn, the gentle, the persecuted—and call them blessed. What kind of man would bless the underdog, the powerless, the sad?

A few verses later I found Jesus redefining the meaning of adultery and telling men not to look lustfully at women. What kind of man was this who understood how degrading and frightening it is for a girl or woman to be ogled, mentally undressed, and raped in men's imaginations?

Soon I came to the story of the woman with the twelve-year continuous menstrual flow. Having recently lived in a culture which, like Jesus', considers menstruating women contaminated and obscene, I again wept as I read of Jesus turning to her as she touched his garment, healing her, and tenderly calling her "daughter."

I read all of Matthew in one sitting. In the next few days I also read Mark, Luke, and John. I was struck with how naturally and freely Jesus related to women of all kinds. In spite of the prevalent Jewish and Gentile cultural and religious bias against women, Jesus didn't treat women any differently from men. He seemed willing to go against conventional ideas and beliefs about women which degraded and isolated and dehumanized them.

I was moved and surprised to notice how Jesus used a

balance of both masculine and feminine imagery in his parables. The woman searching for her lost coin in Luke 15 certainly seemed to represent God. That felt like a love pat to my battered heart. Maybe religious organizations had trouble imaging God in anything but masculine terms, but Jesus seemed capable of doing that.

Although my internalized mental picture of Jesus with his disciples had always consisted of thirteen dark and hairy men, I now was struck with how often women were mentioned in the company of Jesus. Indeed women seemed to be present at all the important events of Jesus' life, death, and resurrection. Surely he knew this would not win him brownie points with the important religious and political men of his day. Still he felt compelled to include them in his ministry and circle of friends.

I tried to imagine how shocking and life-giving Jesus' behavior and attitude must have been for the women with whom he came in contact. I suspected that women were the first really to believe Jesus was the Messiah. Who in that culture, except one come from the heart of God, would have treated them as precious, equally worthy persons?

My own heart was flooded with a deep sense of being loved by Jesus and of falling in love with him once more. As had happened at age eleven when I made my first heartfelt commitment to Jesus, I was again surrounded with a wonderful, mysterious power. This experience of love was truly the gift of hope for which I desperately longed.

I still despair at how the Bible and religious teachings are used to oppress women. I still grieve the absence of women's voices in many biblical stories. I often weep when I think of the many resources wasted because the church does not know how fully to use women's giftedness. Yet I continue to have a deep sense of being loved by

Jesus and of loving him as a natural response to his love. For me this is a life-sustaining gift of grace.   ■

Carolyn Holderread Heggen is a psychotherapist from Albuquerque, New Mexico. She is an elder in her Menno- nite congregation and is author of *Sexual Abuse in Christian Homes and Churches* (Herald Press, 1993). For sheer joy she plays piano and climbs mountains.

8

Streams in the Desert

Anna Kreider Juhnke

PROTESTANTS don't go to the desert to find God, as the early Christian monks used to do. When Jim and I signed up for service in Botswana with Mennonite Central Committee (MCC) in our early thirties, I was looking forward to a service adventure, something beyond the repetitive routine of housework, childcare, and part-time teaching of the same few college courses. I wasn't going to this barren desert country of Africa to seek God, because neither I nor God was lost. I had lived my whole life knowing I was a child of God, trying to be obedient, flourishing in the Christian community.

There was a special joy for us in Botswana. Often I had an exhilarated feeling as I bicycled to school along the dusty roads of our little city before seven in the morning. I received warm greetings from the Botswana women and men on their bicycles and watched the early sun shine on the rocky hills. Even the scrub thornbushes all around us took on a kind of beauty. I felt boundless energy for our new tasks.

And I exhausted myself. I was the competent, highly credentialed teacher, doing all my good work in my own strength, until I was physically and spiritually worn out. I caved in to some minor infection and was sick in bed for six weeks. That was the real desert. Like a lot of other sick people, I felt useless and depressed. Now that I wasn't busy, I had time to pray. But I was too dry to pray. I discovered that I didn't even know how, and that scared me.

Even more frightening was my feeling of having no identity when I couldn't teach, work, and achieve something. I tried to comfort myself by believing that my spiritual state was a result of illness. But deep inside, I suspected that the reverse was true. In any case, the panic of emptiness drove me to seek God in that dry desert country.

As I slowly got well, I began to listen to people who talked about healing, including my charismatic friends. We also started visiting the Apostolic Spiritual Healing Church—a truly African church which believed in healing for the whole person. Whether you were sick or depressed, had lost your job, or were having trouble in your marriage, they laid hands on you and prayed for healing.

But I wasn't free to ask them to lay hands on me and pray for me. These Christians danced and sang because of God's generosity, not because of their own competence or credentials. But I wasn't free to dance with them because I was clumsy, not a good dancer. I realized that I had always managed to avoid situations where I feared I was not competent and in control—like public speaking, for another example. I had been in more of a prison than I had recognized.

But God led me patiently until, at an MCC Easter retreat that year, the cross and resurrection became real for me. The Lord was inviting me to die to my old self, to nail my competence and credentials on the cross and be free to live by God's grace. Suddenly, as in an old Wesley hymn, "My chains fell off, my heart was free; I rose, went forth and followed thee."

The feeling of grace and peace continued with me on the following day when all the petrol stations were closed and we ran out of gas on the way home. While Jim hitched a ride, I sat on the dusty roadside telling stories to our two little children, my heart brimming with joy.

Life felt different. I could be spontaneous with people. I danced in church, and it was okay to be absurdly awkward. I agreed to speak to the student body in chapel, and it was okay to feel my knees knocking. Salvation was happening in that thorny, desert country, as in the words of Isaiah 35:6.

> Then the lame shall leap like a deer,
>   and the tongue of the speechless sing for joy.
> For waters shall break forth in the wilderness
>   and streams in the desert.

Unfortunately, when I came back home to the United States, I slipped slowly back over the years into the shell of supercompetent teacher as my main identity. That put a lot of psychological pressure on me—and a lot more on my students. But somehow I didn't realize how destructive I was to my students, how terrorized some of them felt in my classes.

Finally came a semester as barren and rocky as any desert. A student friend of mine confronted me, speaking the truth in love. I was shattered. With shame I asked the campus pastor to interview some of my students and help me understand what was going wrong. It was hard to confess that teaching was the most unredeemed area of my life, that my "competence" was blocking Christ from speaking through me or using me.

Painfully I surrendered the broken pieces of my self-confidence to God, praying for just enough grace to get through each day. At times that year I thought it would be easier to quit teaching than let God mend what was broken, including my reputation, in whatever time that would take.

In fact it did take several years for the joy to come back into teaching, for me to be able to concentrate on my students instead of thinking, "Oh, no, what am I doing wrong now?" But because of that healing in the desert of Botswana, I knew that God's grace would see me through this new desert stage of my journey. When the African-American students sang the gospel song, "I don't believe he brought me this far to leave me," I could feel the "amen."

I am grateful that God gave me those experiences of spiritual brokenness and healing early enough that I didn't have to cope with them at the time both my sister and I were diagnosed with cancer. This time the prayers and love of the community provided strength I hadn't believed possible. A friend who had lived with cancer left me a note at the hospital before my kidney surgery, encouraging me to see cancer as a pilgrimage. So that night I memorized part of a pilgrimage psalm:

> Blessed are those whose strength is in you,
>   who have set their hearts on pilgrimage.
> As they pass through the Valley of Baca,
>   they make it a place of springs;
>   the autumn rains also cover it with pools.
> They go from strength to strength
>   till each appears before God in Zion.
>   (Psalm 84:5-7 NIV)

Water in the desert . . . springs and streams of it. My sister Sara's cancer quickly worsened, but with calm courage she prepared to appear before God in Zion. Both of us were held up by praying friends and by God's grace. For me it was an almost physical sense of being lifted into the stream of healing power. Despite the pain and the grief, there was a radiance and goodness surrounding this wilderness pilgrimage that stayed with me for a long time.

Ten happy years passed, including a sabbatical year of teaching in China. I thought the cancer was gone. It wasn't.

At the end of 1992, it showed up again in my pancreas. A far more dangerous surgery would be necessary to try to buy another good decade by removing my pancreas and related organs.

We had a very tense Christmas that year, thinking about the surgery at the end of the month at the Mayo Clinic in Minnesota. Two days before Jim and I left for Minnesota, our pastors and close friends at Bethel College Mennonite Church came to our home. They led us in an anointing service and claimed the power of God's healing love on our behalf. It was a wonderful gift. We did feel the power of God's love filling us. We flew north in strength.

I told the surgeon that many people were praying for him. Dr. Thompson answered, "And I will be praying for you." That was somehow a confirmation that I was surrounded by God's love. Dr. Thompson operated on me till ten o'clock at night, and he must have been exhausted. But God was with him and me and with Jim and the other family members who waited and prayed at the hospital. I not only survived, but all my reengineered digestive systems worked! It still seems a miracle.

This time the lonely pilgrimage had been the long months of testing and decisions before the surgery. But the nine months of recovery, when I was too weak to teach, were not a desert of emptiness and lost identity. I experienced a garden of flowers, filled with the love and kindness of many Christian friends.

After a couple of months, I returned to my Thursday morning prayer group of faithful prayer veterans. They had supported me through both cancer crises, and their singing always lifted my spirit. Each season and activity as I returned to it had a new radiance. Teaching again in the fall was a special gift; each colleague and student was a gift. I felt surrounded by love.

It's not all roses. By now some of the glow has gone out

of teaching again. I live with the knowledge that there is no chemotherapy or radiation that works on renal cell carcinoma as backup for my surgery. I now am diabetic, daily aware of the fragile chemistry of my body and of the mysteries of the immune system I'm depending on to suppress new cancer growth. I think often of Psalm 84. I am going "from strength to strength" now, but I'm aware of the end of the pilgrimage, "appearing before God in Zion." When I get there, I can thank God for experiences of grace in desert times, each preparing me for the next stage of the journey. Indeed, I can give thanks now. ■

Anna Kreider Juhnke teaches English at Bethel College, North Newton, Kansas. She and her husband, Jim, have a married daughter and a son who recently returned from service with Peace Corps in Swaziland, Africa. She has frequently led travel courses in England and has taught in Botswana and China. Anna has served on the General Board of the General Conference Mennonite Church and as chair of Mennonite Central Committee, U.S.

9

God's Grace Is Sufficient for Me

Alan Kreider

IN 1962, at the time of the Cuban missile crisis, I was a twenty-year-old graduate student at Princeton University. I had come there ambitious for success, but things were not going according to plan. I was afraid; the spiraling global crisis terrified me. Having just experienced a broken engagement, I was confused, unhappy with the way I had behaved, and emotionally exhausted.

And I was not doing well academically. An economic history professor, whose public personality was cuttingly brilliant and who scared me deeply, had just told the class that my first seminar paper was "a good undergraduate presentation." I took to heart his apparent scorn. As far as I was concerned, all things seemed to be working together for ill.

The nights were the worst for me. Going to sleep was difficult. Waking up at 3:00 a.m. was easy. I was a Christian, having been baptized eleven years earlier, so as I lay in my bed I would try to pray. I had been attending the University Chapel, where the Scriptures were powerfully read and the organ was played by an artist whose records I had collected, but I was inwardly disoriented. How distant God seemed.

One night I sensed that I was at the end of my resources. I was in bed, tossing from side to side, sweating profusely, tormented by fears both rational and irrational. Was I cracking up? Did it matter?

Suddenly the phone rang. To my astonishment, it was my mother. "Are you all right, Alan? I feel troubled about you." My parents were frugal. Long-distance phoning was something that wealthier people did. Except that, on this occasion, Mother knew that she must break precedent, and my homesick inner self wept in gratitude.

Within an hour the phone rang again. This time it was John Mosemann, the pastor of my home church, who happened to be in New York City. He would be in Princeton the next day and wondered whether I would have time to see him. The intuition of my mother, the praying and listening presence of a man who had ministered the mystery of God to me, and the "coincidence" of it all—it was amazing to me.

It was not that I suddenly started feeling all right; it was not that mental sharpness suddenly replaced my confusion; it was not even that I thought I would *live*—at that stage the geopolitical muddle was such that anything could have happened to us all. It was rather that, somehow, God was there, in the midst of the pain, telling me that loving arms were surrounding me, so it was safe to die —or live! I began to sleep at night.

The following Sunday morning, as the missile crisis was reaching its peak, I attended the University Chapel. I don't remember the sermon. I do remember singing Luther's "A Mighty Fortress Is Our God" as I had never sung it before. "Let goods and kindred go, this mortal life also, The body they may kill, God's truth abideth still. His kingdom is forever." And as we flooded out of chapel into a sunny noon-time, the word was quickly passed around that Khrushchev had agreed to withdraw the Soviet missiles and that the crisis was passing.

The rest of my year at Princeton was tough, but my life

began to come together. Once again able to sleep and think, I began to do better in exams and presentations, even for the man who so terrified me. I relaxed and made some friends. I read the Psalms and prayed.

Of one thing I was sure. I had been through a life-threatening crisis and God had saved me. God had reached into my helplessness and had helped me. It was as if God had said, "[I] will fight for you, and you have only to keep still" (Exod. 14:14). God, I felt, had given me a personal exodus. Passages of Scripture came to speak directly to me: God had called me by name (Isa. 43:1), and lovingly had consecrated me before I was born (Jer. 1:5).

I knew that I had done nothing to deserve this. I sensed that, had I relied on my own strength in my tailspin, I would have spun out of graduate school into confusion and personal disarray. But I was saved, rescued, not by works lest I should boast, but by grace. So when I retell to myself the story of my life, I do so with deep thanksgiving. I cannot judge other people whose lives have disintegrated or gone in other directions, for I know that my own life is a gift from God who has loved me. When I think of grace, therefore, I think first of all of God's grace of *rescue*.

I also think of God's grace of *provision*. In the thirty-two years since the Cuban missile crisis, my life has gone in different directions than I had anticipated. I finished my graduate studies and began teaching history at Goshen College in my home town in Indiana; I thought I would spend my life there. I enjoyed that life and, I believe, could have continued to find meaning in it. But another direction opened up which seemed to my wife, Eleanor, and me to be God's calling—work as missionaries in England, a country which for centuries had been "Christian" but was now, like much of the West, becoming materialistic, despirited and cynical.

This call was not easy for me to accept, for I have had a

painful history of feeling marginal ever since I was a fifth grader and my family moved to Japan. From Parkside School in Goshen, where people knew what a Mennonite was, I moved to a U.S. Army school in Tokyo, where I found it hard to explain to soldiers' children what rank my father had!

Since our move to England, I've sometimes found it hard to live where "Mennonite" may be confused with "Mormon" (some North American sect beginning with M), where developing supportive networks of people who share our convictions take much time, and where it is hard to structure my life and predict outcomes. How much I've longed for the grace of a college dean to tell me what to do! And yet, as I look back on twenty-plus years of life in England, I am full of gratitude. For the God who has led us into insecurity has graciously taken care of us. "Do not be afraid, . . . for it is your Father's good pleasure to give you the kingdom" (Luke 12:32).

God's gifts of provision have been richly varied, and I must be selective. I think of God's sheer fidelity to me during a time in the early 1980s when I was making a mess of relationships. In grace God gave both the strength to endure and, through wise friends in the Post Green Community, new perspectives on myself, on the necessity of listening, and on prayer. I think of God's grace in providing sisters and brothers, both in the London Mennonite Centre and in the Wood Green Mennonite Church, who have supported me and spoken truth to me.

I think of breakthroughs, so hard to predict, in which God did something new. Eight years ago Stuart Murray, leader of a rapidly growing new church in a tough area of London where most churches were closing, heard my missionary colleague Wally Fahrer speak. Wally stated that God had poured out the Holy Spirit in charismatic renewal, not just to give people enjoyable experiences, but to empower them to follow Jesus in a more radically faithful way.

Stuart, a highly rational person, was uncharacteristically moved emotionally. In response to what he believes was a message from God, he has changed his thinking and his life. He has written a Ph.D. thesis on Anabaptist interpretation of Scripture, has become an influential teacher of church planting and evangelism (which he refuses to segregate from discipleship), and is a prime mover in a growing Anabaptist Network that is transforming Christians and churches throughout the United Kingdom. Who, a decade ago, could have predicted what is happening? God is gracious!

At times, God's providing grace has expressed itself in improbable, even miraculous, forms. Two weeks ago Ellie and I, on a long-distance train journey, were having a cup of tea in the station cafe in Birmingham while changing trains. Suddenly I looked up. "Wilbert!" Who should be there but Wilbert Shenk, our friend and colleague of many years who was not in Indiana where he teaches, but travelling between missiological conferences in England and Scotland. In our half-hour together, Wilbert once more was able to affirm us in a new project that we were undertaking. How improbable our meeting was, and how generous the God who enabled it!

I think of our wise sister Sharon Stinson who, knowing that we were hunting for a place for a sabbatical in 1984, said with spiritual authority, "Come to York." Just the right house was available. Little did she, or we, know how formative and healing our months there would be for Ellie; our son, Andrew; and me as individuals and as a family.

More recently Sharon phoned me and said, "You must go on retreat. There is an Ignatian retreat for peacemakers. Go on it." I went, and found Jesus there, asking me probing questions and speaking loving truth to me. Repeatedly, through Sharon's intervention, God has led to sources of new energy which enable me to give to God and the world the gifts that I tend to disparage.

As a marginal person and outsider, I have struggled throughout my adult life to believe that I have contributions to make. A major source of grace for me has been friends who have believed in me—and in us Mennonites—and who have urged us to speak our word boldly. I think of Jim Punton, who proposed that our infant Mennonite book service perform the grown-up task of running the bookstall at the Greenbelt Christian Arts Festival; or of John Stott, who at the height of the arms race thought that I could debate with a general; or of Larry Miller, who has kept opening new horizons of God's call.

Above all, I think of Eleanor, who not only gives me the grace of encouragement but who has emerged as a major synergist in my life. We love this New Testament term "co-workers" (*synergoi*, Rom. 16:3; Phil. 4:3; etc.) which gives expression to our experience that, in studying and speaking together, two people can unleash a disproportionate amount of creative energy.

I celebrate all of these as examples of God's gracious reality. And the celebration is indispensable. I find that when I "forget all [God's] benefits" (Ps. 103:2), I get in trouble in characteristic ways—self-doubt and depression. So I try to remember, primarily by writing. In my journal I enter a variety of things: dreams, times when I have seen something new that has seized my imagination, occasions on which I got angry (what is the anger telling me?). But especially I record things that seem to me to be actions of God, the moments of "coincidence" that I interpret as miracles of provision, the events of breakthrough and new possibility, the reassurances of God's presence and faithfulness amidst humdrum or dryness.

When I'm discouraged I reread this journal; it nurtures

me to retell the story of salvation as I have experienced it. My daily prayer, then, gives thanks for this story and prays that it may continue: "Give us this day our daily bread." And as God gives me daily manna, I delight in remembering God's grace of provision.

So I have known God's rescuing and providing grace; I have also known the grace of God's *pardon*: "He has rescued us from the power of darkness and transferred us into the kingdom of his beloved Son, in whom we have redemption, the forgiveness of sins" (Col. 1:13-14). At Princeton I knew that the God who had rescued me had also accepted me. God loved me even though he knew that priorities weren't right in my life.

It had mattered to me to dress well—I wanted to appear sophisticated; it had also been important to me to be successful in the world's eyes. Through God's loving acceptance I found these receding as ephemeral; God was forgiving me for preoccupations that were not consistent with the kingdom. The result was a new desire on my part to have fellowship with God which led to devotional disciplines. "I love the Lord, because he has heard my voice" (Ps. 116:1).

But as time passed deeper levels emerged which I could not yet properly articulate; I have continued to struggle with these. Spiritual writer Gerald Hughes calls these "layers of atheism"; when one through grace peels one off, there is a new subtler one waiting to reveal itself. So it has been with me. It was one thing for me to be forgiven for materialism and over-ambition, and to be set free for a more trusting lifestyle and an eccentric career path. It has been altogether more difficult for me to realize that my sin is not primarily things that I *do* but rather things that I, in my unhealed inner recesses, still *am*.

At times I recognize in myself the struggling idealist. As a Christian I have been nourished by the writings and

examples of sisters and brothers in the early church and in
the Anabaptist movement. They have shown me that a
biblical radicalism is possible, that Christian discipleship
can address the addictions and compulsions of any age—
domination, discontent, violence. I long to see the church
renewed and living like Jesus; I long to see the world become a place in which justice and shalom embrace.

And yet, I struggle. In a world that is so comprehensively in trouble, why are God's people—why am I—so
thoughtless, so conventional, so accepting of the world's
wisdom? Why is it proving so difficult to give birth to a
more radical and communitarian form of church, in which
I deeply believe? Why does "renewal"—whether charismatic or contemplative—so often produce, not grace-
bearing disciples, but spiritual consumers or "retreat-
house junkies"? In our civilization, is it our wealth that
"choke(s) the word" (Matt. 13:22)? Or is it deeply rooted
secularism?

In my experience, God has many ways of freeing me
from the idealist's struggles. One way is to meet new believers whose lives have been comprehensively changed
by God's grace in Jesus. What tonic they are! Getting out of
my rut and meeting people—gentle evangelists and persistent peace workers, Anabaptist Baptists and "More-with-
Less Episcopalians," people of prayer and people of inven-
tive discipleship, perhaps above all Christians from poorer
countries—these people humble and excite me.

So do churches in many parts of the world in which
there is innovation and fidelity. Events on the global scale
can exhilarate: the South African elections have been a
huge gift of grace which has given me hope for other
places, such as Northern Ireland whose problems have
seemed equally insoluble.

I struggle, in short, when I keep my eyes fixed on my
ideals and lose sight of God. I wither inwardly when I

complain that the mustard seed is small, instead of seeing life and exclaiming, "Hey, this is going to be a big tree!" (Matt. 13:32).

My ideals can be idols, and I struggle until God lovingly dethrones them by defogging my vision and leading me to repentance. If my sight is clear and accompanied by thanks and praise, God can purify my longings for justice and reconciliation and, I believe, even use them.

I also recognize lurking in myself the perfectionist. My assignment in England has been a varied one, in which I often have had to speak about many subjects without adequate preparation. This is exciting but also scary.

I'm often hard on myself, and I fret about my inability to do a "decent job" on this or that. My graduate-school training is not a help here: "What will scholars think about this, Kreider? Can you footnote it?" A spiritual director once advised me, when I was fretting about being inadequate for a new kind of assignment: "Relax, Alan. Just offer them yourself."

I want what I do for God to be my best, and I delight in careful research and writing. But my "decent job" must be determined by what genuinely serves God, and that may require that I hazard a hunch or skimp on a footnote. At the root of my perfectionist strivings, I sense, is a self-protectiveness which breaks the first commandment, which denies God the right to be God and shackles me by pedantry.

Only grace can overcome this. I have found grace in the faith of others. I have often found myself being literally carried by others whose vision of God is profounder, whose love is more intense, and who have believed in God (and in me) even when I haven't. How freely God's grace is mediated through the multi-gifted body of Christ!

In my experience, "spiritual friends," who have shared with me a commitment to listen and pray, have been particular grace-bearers. I have also found grace in the Scriptures, which speak truth with an authority which I recognize because the best in my experience gives deep assent.

So when I hear Jesus saying to Paul, and to me, "My grace is sufficient for you, for power is made perfect in weakness" (2 Cor. 12:9), my heart responds with praise to the wondrous God whose victories have rarely come about by conventional means. The response to pardon, genuinely appropriated, is always praise.

It was almost a decade ago that I discovered yet another source of grace—the gift of *Shabbat*. I resisted a legalistic determination of this day or that as my Sabbath; and I continue to struggle to be faithful to the vision of a day in the week not dedicated to productive work. Good things to do crowd in upon me, and I at times respond to the demands and deadlines with a weak will. But I know that, for me at least, a day of rest is a source of grace.

God knows I need to pray and play. Only as I rest, in stillness, in attentiveness, in prayerfulness, can I realize what God has done for me. When I rest, I read the Bible, some spiritual writing, or my journal, thereby reorienting myself to the gracious presence of the God I worship. "Come to me," Jesus beckons, "all you that are weary and carrying heavy burdens, and I will give you rest" (Matt 11:28).

Resting, for me, includes activities that are playful, intentionally unproductive. God desires that we delight in beauty and creativity. I'm not a hobby gardener nor a birdwatcher, but for me resting means walking in the countryside, savoring nature, or listening to Mozart.

Praying and playing do not directly address the needs of the world; but such a day is essential if I am to appropriate grace. Only through *Shabbat* can I say to God, "The world is in your hands. You are sovereign. You bring the kingdom." When God's kingdom comes, it will be the result, not of my works, but of God's grace.

On my wall are three visual images. All of them are depictions of the hands of God; and all of them remind me of grace. There is a Taizé stained glass window with God's hands surrounding Isaac—the grace of rescue. There is a Chartres sculpture of God's hands fashioning humanity—the grace of the provision of life. And there is the image that I most cherish: the Rembrandt drawing of Jesus, walking on the water, whose hands reach down to the disciple who was at first so bold and then so quick to sink—the grace of pardon and rescue for faithful discipleship. "Gracious is the Lord, and righteous . . . when I was brought low, he saved me. Return, O my soul, to your rest, for the Lord has dealt bountifully with you" (Ps. 116:5-7). ∎

Alan Kreider was born in Indiana but spent his formative early-teen years in Tokyo. His historical studies at Goshen (Indiana) College, Princeton University, and Harvard University prepared him admirably for college teaching, but since 1974 he has done work with the Mennonite Board of Missions in England. He has ministered among international students, helped found the first (since 1575) Mennonite congregation in England, and been involved in the development of the London Mennonite Centre as a place of teaching, Anabaptist resourcing, prayer, and hospitality. Since 1991 he has been based elsewhere, for four years in Manchester and beginning in mid-1995 in Oxford; in both places he has dealt with favorite themes—the Early Church as a resource for renewal today, and Christianity and culture. With his wife Eleanor he travels widely to speak and to help develop a UK-wide Anabaptist Network.

10

All Shall Be Well

Marlene Kropf

OUTSIDE my classroom a gunshot exploded. "How will I protect the students?" I thought numbly. Concrete block walls with many openings for ventilation provided little protection against a violent gunman.

I tried to pray, but no thoughts or words came. God seemed a million miles away. I wondered who was being killed and how long it would be until the gunman broke into our classroom. I wondered why I couldn't pray.

In 1976, as part of a service assignment with Mennonite Central Committee, I was teaching English at St. Andrew Technical High School in Kingston, Jamaica. Although I loved teaching, I dreaded the daily drive to school through the violent streets of Kingston. Some city streets had been closed to vehicles because of danger from random gunfire.

I remember telling someone one day, "What bothers me most is the fear that I will die a totally senseless death —shot by a stray bullet. I can understand dying for a reason or a cause, but I can't bear the thought of being gunned down just because I happened to be walking down the street on a sunny day."

That morning in my classroom the sound of shots eventually subsided. Without seeming disturbed, students went back to their work. I was puzzled by their calm response to danger. Then I realized that the intrusion of gunfire was a far too ordinary event in the ghettos where they lived. What completely unnerved me was a daily reality with which they had learned to cope.

But my peace had been broken. A policeman had been wantonly killed in the field beside my school. And with his death, a dark, swirling fear rose to the surface of my brain and refused to go away. For the several months remaining in my term of service, I lived with an increasing sense of agitation and eventual exhaustion.

Why couldn't I pray in a moment of great danger? And why was I frozen with fear? How can a person who has grown up in a Christian family and in the church suddenly be so bereft of spiritual resources? Was my faith a fraud? Where was God when I most needed a refuge?

During the next year I struggled to make sense of the avalanche of questions released by that day's events. I found some comfort when I read a similar story in Gail Sheehy's best-selling book *Passages: Predictable Crises in Adult Life* (New York: E. P. Dutton, 1976). After witnessing senseless killing in the streets of Derry in Northern Ireland while working on a journalism assignment, she wrote,

> Some dark switch was thrown, and a series of weights began to roll across my brain like steel balls. . . . The world was negligent. Thirteen could perish, or thirteen thousand, I could perish, and tomorrow it would all be beside the point.
> As I joined the people lying on their stomachs, a powerful idea took hold: *No one is with me. No one can keep me safe. There is no one who won't ever leave me alone.*
> I had a headache for a year. (pp. 4-5.)

I learned from Sheehy's book that at age thirty-three I had been hurled into midlife crisis. Faced with my own fragile mortality, I discovered that the foundation of my faith was tottering. Though I had been an active Christian and church member for many years and could discuss the idea of trust in God, I didn't have a deep, abiding, personal sense of being safe in God's hands.

Several steps were important in reclaiming my spiritual health. I joined a small group of people who, with our pastor, were exploring the emotional foundations of faith. A memory which surfaced during this time was the devastation I felt at age three when a diphtheria epidemic swept through our little community and took three of my childhood friends, one a cousin. Thirty years later, I grieved their deaths and experienced healing of that childhood trauma.

I began reading about faith development. The work of James W. Fowler, eventually published in *Stages of Faith* (San Francisco: Harper & Row, 1981), was crucial in helping me understand the typical stages of spiritual growth and the obstacles which can stunt or hinder maturity.

At the same time I began, somewhat tentatively, to read the writings of Morton Kelsey and other spiritual guides who introduced me to the world of contemplative spirituality. I remember sitting in a sun-filled library one day reading Kelsey's *Encounter with God* (Minneapolis: Bethany Fellowship, 1972) and being awakened to the reality that God wants to meet and know me. I felt I was being converted from a faith mainly of the mind to a faith that included heart and body as well.

But the most important step I took was to learn the disciplines of silence and contemplative prayer. In 1978 I was invited to participate in a three-day silent retreat. Fearful yet expectant, I opened myself to listen to God in ways I had never experienced. To my surprise and delight, I met a gentle, compassionate God in the silence, a God who called me to trust and friendship.

At the end of the retreat, we were instructed to go home and practice "praying the Scriptures" for at least six months before speaking too quickly of our experience to others. Though I couldn't resist telling a few close friends of my discovery, I did submit to the discipline of practicing what I had learned. For nearly two years, I prayed the Psalms and the Gospels on a regular basis and opened myself to transformation. Out of that experience, others asked to join me on the spiritual journey, and eventually I acquired formal training for guiding people to meet God through the ministry of spiritual direction.

The journey that began in a Jamaican classroom on a hot spring day has not been easy. Learning to listen to God and to trust that, in the words of the hymn, "Jesus will not fail me," has cost me the illusion that I am self-sufficient and can control my life. Henri Nouwen gave me words for such a conversion when he wrote about the long journey from the "house of fear to the house of love."

My conservative religious background, though it provided me with many gifts, did not give me what I needed most to grow toward God: a simple, secure confidence that nothing I could do—or not do—could separate me from God's love (Rom. 8:38-39). What I received instead was conditional religion. If I did certain things and didn't do certain other things, I would be acceptable to God.

Such distorted thinking always leads to fear. Henri Nouwen says, "Most of us people of the twentieth century live in the house of fear most of the time" (*Lifesigns* [Garden City, N.Y.: Doubleday, 1986], p. 15). However, we are created for love—not fear. Intimacy with God cannot coexist with fear. Nor can we freely open our hands to others as long as we are full of fear.

On the journey from fear to love, Julian of Norwich has been my most trustworthy human guide. A fourteenth-century woman of prayer, Julian experienced a series of visions in which she was shown the profound goodness and love of God. Her book called *Revelations of Divine Love* reflects the reality of her life lived in the midst of a violent world filled with death. Yet beneath and above and beyond all she knows and sees, Julian perceives a deeper mystery—that love is our Lord's meaning. At the heart of reality is a faithful God who tenderly loves all that has been made and who promises that "all shall be well, and all manner of things shall be well" (Garden City, N.Y., Doubleday, 1977, p. 124).

Slowly, painfully, joyfully, the conviction that all shall be well has come to dwell in my blood and bones. Though I have no way of knowing what dangers and distress lie ahead, I am convinced, with Paul, that nothing "will be able to separate us from the love of God" (Rom. 8:39). Such good news offers great joy and opens the way for me to join with God's creative, loving, healing purposes in the world. ∎

Marlene Kropf is employed as minister of worship and spirituality at Mennonite Board of Congregational Ministries, Elkhart, Indiana. She also serves as adjunct faculty in worship and spiritual formation at Associated Mennonite Biblical Seminary, Elkhart. As part of her work at the seminary, she serves as spiritual director for individual students. She is married to Stanley E. Kropf, and they are parents of two young adult children.

11

Stranger on the Grate

Earl Martin

SOMETIMES it happens when you least expect it.

This cute little experiment is taking a nasty turn. What did I expect anyway? Maybe I should have stuck a couple twenties in my shoe, so I could get a room in a flophouse. But at this moment there seems no way of going back.

I know I can't make it through this near freezing night in the open, like the guys on the benches in the park.

Exhausted, and feeling the onset of a quiet desperation, I slump onto a steam grate on the sidewalk beside a glimmering office building. Time to warm the bones. On the grate beside me, the crumpled form of a man snores evenly in the night air.

Across the street a white Lincoln Continental stretch limousine pulls up to the spotless Four Seasons Hotel. A glamorous couple gets out and disappears gaily into their five-starred bliss.

It's like the one dude said in the park an hour earlier when I asked him how he felt having no place to stay while all these fancy hotels and heated office buildings towered above us.

"Hey, man, you just gotta accept it. In this society, *some's in; some's out.*"

Only then do I realize it. While some heat is coming from the adjacent grate, my grate is cold. I drop my head onto my knees in discouragement. Dare I lie beside the man on the next grate? Would that be violating his space?

Suddenly I sense an awesome presence above me. Tense, ready to spring, I lift my eyes. The visitor is big. Black beard. Piercing eyes looking down.

Wanting to scream, I manage a decently casual, "Oh, hello there."

"What you doing here, fella?"

"Just trying to get a little rest, sir. Uh, and may I know your name?"

"Call me Sam. Where you live, fella"?

I decide the true story might be the most believable . . . and hence the safest. "Well, I tell you, I'm from Lancaster, sixty miles west. I'm attending a conference here in Philadelphia and decided to check out, to see how things were on the street scene."

"You got a *job*, don't you. And a home and you got money, I bet."

The mention of money scares me. "You're right there, sir. I've got a family and a decent job. Sure, I earn money, but I left my wallet back at the church where we're having the conference."

"What's this conference all about?"

"It's about the Philippines. You know, that country in Asia. I used to work there. Right now there's a lot of fighting going on and thousands of families have to flee their homes. The military calls them rebels and drives them out of their homes. And our government is paying a lot of money to support that military. So at this conference we're trying to understand the connections between homeless people here in the U.S. and the families made homeless in the Philippines. I decided to see how it would be to spend a night on the streets."

Sam eyes me coolly, then explodes, "That's bull----. That's so much bull----."

He steps over to the adjacent grate, grouses at the sleeping man to move over, and lies down beside him. As he puts his head back to sleep, he mutters again, "Bull----."

Now fully awake, I realize this frigid grate will never get me through the night. I frantically pace back toward City Hall. I stop in front of the Cathedral of St. Peter and St. Paul.

Ah, yes, the church. A sanctuary. Haven for the outcast. I walk up the marble steps and bang on the doors. Huge doors. Ornate doors. Locked doors. No response. Of course, stupid! Who ever heard of an unlocked church? Whoa . . . nothing like desperation to awaken a touch of cynicism.

Back on the street, I ask other homeless fellows if there's a shelter where I might stay.

"Yeah, at Ridge and Thirteenth," one man tells me. "But the lice are bad."

Lice or no lice, it's a matter of survival now. It's past midnight. I walk through darkened alleys and between abandoned buildings that feel like the valley of the shadow.

Finally I find the shelter on Ridge and Thirteenth and bang on the door. The guy in the lobby opens the door a crack.

"Full up, man. No room."

"Please, sir, how about just sleeping on the floor in the hallway."

"Sorry, fire regulations. No room. Try the shelter at Spring Garden and Twentieth."

Half hour later at Spring Garden and Twentieth I see a church. Thank God, at least one church is worth its salt. A guy is replacing a broken lightbulb near the door.

"Please, sir, could I stay in your shelter tonight? I'm a bit desperate."

"Sorry, we're full. Try the Thirtieth Street station, Amtrak, the upper platform. Sometimes the police don't run you out of there."

It's one-thirty a.m. as I trudge desperately down a side street. My eye catches the name on the lighted glass door, "Ninth Police District."

In the lobby I implore, "Excuse me, officer, do you know where a fellow can spend the night?"

"Shelter on Ridge Avenue," the officer fires back.

"I tried there and they're full."

"Shelter at that church at Spring Garden and Twentieth."

"Tried there too, sir. Also full."

"Then, buddy, you'll just have to pull up a space there on the floor in the hallway."

I slump to the floor. It's warm enough that I can use my overcoat for a pillow. Exhausted, I'm out till a polished boot is nudging my shoulder at six in the morning.

"Get on the move, guys." As I try to collect my wits and stumble out, I notice another homeless man had joined me in the hallway in the night.

In the early morning, grateful to have made it through the night, I head back toward Center City. Up ahead, a plume of white steam billows up from a small circular grate in the sidewalk. I see a man standing, shrouded by the steam. He looks like a saint on the Mount of Transfiguration or a bearded Moses being led by his pillar of cloud.

"Hey, man, I'm hungry," a voice calls from the cloud.

It's Sam! He recognizes me. We walk together to Center City. He tells me he is a welder, lost his job, and landed on the streets. He leads me to the glass-paneled Tourist Center across from City Hall. The elevated walkway around the circular building is covered with piles of blankets and large refrigerator boxes occupied with still sleeping men and—I'm startled to notice—a few women.

One pile of blankets with its sleeping occupant underneath is crowned with a black leather book: Holy Bible.

Sam seems to know everybody. He bangs on the cardboard cartons. "Got any food in there?" Not all the replies are polite. Finally one friend responds to Sam's cry by thrusting his arm out through the blankets. He is holding a large muffin.

I know what is coming. Sam will wolf down that muffin, and it will be gone in a flash—but no!

Sometimes it happens when you least expect it.

Sam held the muffin in his rough black hands. The sun stopped in its tracks. The axis of the universe started to turn around that muffin in Sam's hands.

At that moment, Sam closed his eyes and bowed his head. The clouds above the City Hall lightened and—can I trust my memory?—I heard a far off voice sounding out, "This is my son. Behold, my beloved son!"

And when Sam raised his eyes, he took the muffin, broke it in two, and gave one half to me.

"Here, man, let's eat."

As we stood under the open sky and ate together, it almost seemed again I heard that voice:

> "This is my body which is given for you,
>   do this in remembrance of me . . .
>   do this in remembrance of me." ∎

Earl Martin normally sleeps in his home in Ephrata, Pennsylvania, with his wife, Pat Hostetter Martin. They and their three children have worked numerous years in Asia with Mennonite Central Committee. Earl now does communications work and storytelling with MCC.

12

God Looks Like Russell

Lynn A. Miller

THINKING back on it, when I showed up on his doorstep in the fall of 1970, I was probably Russell's worst nightmare. It would be hard to imagine two people with more different value systems. Russell had been a stalwart member of the Zion Hill Church of the Brethren in Columbiana, Ohio, longer than I had been alive. He and his wife, Kathryn, were on the deacon board.

He was a craftsman, a carpenter, and a mason. By himself he could build a house from the hole in the ground right up to the ridgecap. And most important, Russell was what you could call reliably conservative. The largest collection of literature in Russell's house was at least twenty years worth of *Reader's Digest*.

I was the exact opposite. I was a skeptic when it came to religion, especially Christianity. In my nine years, two months, and four days service in the United States Navy, I had met far too many people who had Christ on their lips and murder on their hearts. I was not interested in joining the world's largest group of hypocrites.

When I left the navy in 1968, fleeing from any further direct participation in the legalized madness called the Vietnam War, I was trying to become a late-blooming flower child. I had almost missed the sixties, and I was catching up.

I adopted the long hair, outrageous clothes, and hip attitude I admired in the hippies I met on the University of

Washington campus in Seattle. Unlike one current politician my age, I did inhale when I tried marijuana—and loved it!

Perhaps to atone for my personal sins in our national warfare, I jumped into the antiwar movement with both feet. When the news of the Cambodian invasion and the subsequent Kent State killings hit Seattle, I took to the streets with the rest of the outraged students. Suffice to say, Russell and I couldn't have been more different.

So why was that a problem? I probably was different from at least a million people in this country. But by some strange quirk of fate, or more accurately, the even stranger quirk in human experience called "falling-in-love," I was Russell's son-in-law.

In 1964, Russell's oldest child, Linda Jean Pine, left the familiar confines of northeastern Ohio and drove to California looking for something different. She and a fellow nurse at the hospital in Warren, Ohio, decided in the wee hours of one long night shift that they needed to plow new ground. They resigned, packed up Linda's 1962 Buick Special convertible, and headed for the place where having a convertible made a lot more sense.

When they got to the West Coast, they first checked out the city of the Golden Gate Bridge. Although there were any number of jobs for nurses from Ohio, there weren't any apartments in San Francisco that two nurses with two jobs could afford. So they headed south to Long Beach where one of them had a distant cousin. On their second day there, they both found jobs and an affordable apartment close by. But then, one fateful evening soon after their arrival, they made the mistake of visiting the cousin, who lived in an apartment upstairs from something they never knew existed—a "snake ranch."

A "snake ranch" is an unofficial navy term for an apartment rented by sailors, who otherwise would return in the wee hours of the morning to their bunks on the ships up at the Naval Station. This particular snake ranch was a two-bedroom apartment inhabited by me and two navy buddies. We were in three different duty sections, which meant one of us was always on duty and therefore staying on the ship overnight. That was why we needed only two bedrooms, the all-important "dens" of any snake ranch.

The three of us were all involved in electronics repair and maintenance on our ship. On that fateful day, we received a request from the cousin to come up to her apartment to look at a malfunctioning stereo system. When we arrived we discovered two things. First, the stereo was not seriously damaged. Second, the cousin had company. Sitting on the couch in that apartment were two young women, newcomers to us and, more importantly, potential victims for the bedrooms of the snake ranch below.

But this turned out not to be the normal pursuit-and-conquer routine well practiced by a couple of sailors who had just returned from eight months in the South China Sea. These young ladies were different from the rest we were busy pursuing. And one was particularly interesting to me.

To my embarrassment, I must admit that my first memory of the woman who was soon to be my wife was only of a fuzzy blue shape sitting on the couch with her legs tucked away beneath her. The next day when I called their apartment, I didn't have a clear picture of what her face looked like. I didn't even know what her name was. But God was good. I got the right woman on the phone, one thing led to another, and soon I was Russell Pine's son-in-law.

We were planning to have the wedding in the coming summer of 1965 in Linda's home church in Ohio. But the closer the date came, the more evident it became that we wouldn't have the money necessary to travel to the Midwest for the planned July 10 wedding. So on April 2, to save expenses by living together and to collect the $104 extra pay I would receive by being married, we went to the Candlelight Wedding Chapel on Long Beach Boulevard. For $20 we were made husband and wife. Then in July we traveled to Ohio, where for the first time I met Linda's father, Russell Pine.

Now in 1965 Russell and I were not so different. I was still in the navy, still clean shaven, and still reasonably disciplined. Five years later, however, I was as different from Russell as I could get. What was worse, that difference was about to make a difference. Differences between people don't matter much if they don't live together or if they don't care about the differences. That was the situation between Russell and me until the politically hot summer of 1970. When I joined the nationwide student strike, I lost my tuition, my GI benefits, and my status as a student. In short, something had to go, and it turned out to be me.

Perhaps seeing the future even through letters, Linda's parents had earlier extended a vague invitation for us to "come stay" with them. In the summer of 1970, we put our house up for sale, bought a used GMC step-van, put everything we wanted to keep in it, including the two girls, and headed east toward the promised land called Ohio. The truck was decorated with flower decals covering the rust spots, and was identified on both sides with the sign "THE FREE SPIRIT TINKER AND JUNK COMPANY."

And so it was that Russell was confronted with a long-haired, hippie-freak son-in-law who had his daughter and grandchildren living in a truck.

I expected from Russell exactly what I had experienced during the past several years from most of the "unliberated" people I had met. I expected to be told to get a haircut, to stop smoking, to "straighten up and fly right." Instead, to my shock, I received the opposite. I was loved in spite of who or what I was.

Despite his certain embarrassment, Russell took me into his life, introducing me to his friends, his church, his world. He taught me his trade and put me to work mixing mortar and even laying a few bricks on the new sanctuary of the Zion Hill congregation. I thought at the time that I was working for the church, but later I found out that my wages came out of Russell's pocket.

It wasn't only my physical or financial welfare that Russell was concerned about. He often took me with him on his "deaconing" trips. I remember helping him shovel coal into the basements of widows on small fixed incomes, discovering later that it was Russell who had paid for the coal. And in the six months that God kept Russell and me together, Russell took more than one wandering soul into his life, offering work and friendship to those who had neither.

All this love was offered before any of us deserved it! That is why it comes under the category of grace. For grace is the love we receive before we have earned it. In Romans 5 the apostle Paul is clear about the state we were in when God loved us. "For while we were still weak, at the right time Christ died for the ungodly" (v. 6). "But God proves his love for us in that while we still were sinners Christ died for us" (v. 8). Again, "while we were enemies, we were reconciled to God through the death of his son" (v. 10). In Ephesians 2:4-5, Paul is even more specific about what kind of love this is. "But God, who is rich in mercy, out of the great love with which he loved us even when we were dead through our trespasses, made us alive together with Christ—by grace you have been saved."

That is what Russell was offering to me, love in the midst of my own sins, grace. He offered it because of who he was, not because of what I had become. That is the whole point of what *grace* is and isn't. Grace isn't driven by what the recipient deserves or even needs. Grace is driven by who God is. And God's essential character is one of love and mercy. Grace is a kind of love that is gently offered rather than insisted on. We are free to turn it down, and many do. But grace is often irresistible, especially when it comes through God's people, people like Russell.

Grace also comes with a price. Five years after loving me into the kingdom of God, Russell was killed in the act of offering himself to another lost soul. This stranger didn't recognize God in Russell's behavior, only threat. And when Russell went toward him to make another stranger into a friend, this stranger acted out of his fear. He kidnapped Russell at gunpoint, marched him two miles into the thick hardwood forest near Madison, Ohio, and shot him in the back of the head from a distance of twelve feet.

Russell lost his life trying to make another soul "alive together with him in Christ." This was probably not a great surprise to Russell. For he knew that it was precisely when his Lord was offering his love to a stranger that he died.

So if you get to heaven before I do, look for a short, older fellow wearing those faded gray-and-white striped carpenter's overalls, with a matching engineer's cap, perhaps playing an accordion. If you see someone like that, say hello for me. And don't worry about making a mistake. If it isn't Russell, I suspect it will be God. It would not surprise me at all to find that God looks a lot like those who act like God.   ■

Lynn Miller was born in Peoria, Illinois, in 1941. He lived in nine towns in three countries before leaving home at age seventeen to join the U.S. Navy where he spent about ten years, including two trips to the Vietnam War.

From 1970 to 1982, Lynn had a wide variety of experiences, including two six-month voluntary service assignments, three years with Mennonite Central Committee in Botswana, and another three years combining farming and prison chaplaincy in Illinois. After receiving his M.Div. degree from Associated Mennonite Biblical Seminary (Elkhart, Ind.) in 1985, Lynn pastored the South Union Mennonite Church in West Liberty, Ohio.

Following the publication of his book *Firstfruits Living* (Herald Press, 1991), Lynn accepted an assignment as stewardship teacher for the Churchwide Stewardship Council (Mennonite Church), where he and Linda are on a Mennonite Voluntary Service (MVS) assignment in the East Garfield Park neighborhood. Lynn is married to Linda (Pine). They are the parents of two adult daughters, Lori (Nester) and Liana. They now live in Chicago.

13

Conversion in Midstream

Tom Yoder Neufeld

I GREW UP in a minister's home. I recall telling my father at a revival service at the age of five that I wanted to be a Christian. I have never felt the need to dismiss that experience, even if much more would be needed in the future to equip me with a faith that could cope with adult life. I was baptized at age thirteen, coming to this decision with seriousness and little if any peer pressure. For that experience too I remain grateful.

While I know that my personal identity as a Christian goes back to those early experiences, I also know that I have needed more conversion in the midst of my life as a Christian. One particularly important experience of "conversion in midstream" stands out.

During my university years in Winnipeg in the late 1960s, I found myself seriously questioning my faith, God, and especially the church. The church claimed to be a community of persons who had been changed by faith in Christ. But I often felt that the life people in the church lived looked ordinary and not particularly concerned with injustice, violence, and war. At times it felt like I was learning about justice and peacemaking mostly from people who did not share my faith.

This was a confusing time for me. I recall my interior disposition as being flat. There was little joy and still less certainty, though I was active in both my own congregation and in a Christian student organization. I wondered whether I might be more agnostic than believer.

Then at the end of my undergraduate studies, I was invited to be a youth representative at a congress on evangelism in Ottawa, Ontario, Canada. I participated in the congress with a mix of enjoyment and suspicion. I found various things to criticize, from the way some people talked about faith to the kinds of people I was encountering. I recall especially one person who was not a delegate to the congress. He would sit every day and play his guitar in the lobby of the hotel, hoping for someone's spare sandwich or for a buck to drop into his guitar case. I avoided him.

The congress as a whole ended on a sour note for me. I had heard a lot of what sounded like old well-worn ways of talking about how Christ changes everything. But little of it connected to the issues I thought the church should be speaking to and helping to change—like the war in Vietnam, a major concern for many of us university students at that time.

I had come feeling flat, and I was going to leave even flatter. And now I was going to go on to study theology at Harvard feeling empty and cynical. I had decided to go there mostly because I was afraid of what I would find. But, I figured, there is no sense in having a faith, however troubled, which cannot hold up in what I thought might be a hostile environment. Still, I was a little worried.

But something happened first. Immediately after the congress there was to be a student conference, and I was a delegate. At the first evening meeting there was singing and prayer. Then I saw that hotel lobby panhandler. I wondered who had let him into this conference. This was, after all, a conference for university graduates who had been active as leaders in student groups.

Then I heard him pray. His prayer was simple. I remember it word for word: "Thank you, God, for your beautiful family. Amen." To my surprise, I was suddenly overcome with emotion. Here was someone I had avoided, even looked down on, who had found Christ at an evangelistic rally at the previous congress, the kind of rally I disliked intensely. Now he was thanking God for being part of a beautiful family; I knew I was a sometimes reluctant member of that family.

I began to weep uncontrollably. Not with shame, it turns out but with joy. I had not cried in years, and I had certainly never cried out of sheer exhilaration. Joy at this person's coming to know God. Joy at feeling joy. Joy at being able to cry. Joy at knowing that I too was part of this special family. I remember leaving the room and giving the loudest whoop I could muster in the cool night air. What a way of having God sneak up on me!

The next morning I walked into a communion service late. The speaker was an American, wearing a powder blue sport jacket and big black, wing-tip shoes; his hair was slicked back with Brylcreem. His appearance alone would turn off any Vietnam War protester. And I was turned off. But then he said something like this: "The only reason we can dare to follow Christ is that God loves us. There are no guarantees beyond that."

The joy of the previous evening gave way to deep seriousness. Again I felt addressed by God with a directness that was almost infuriating. God's directness went right past my prejudices, my defenses. For some years God had been at arm's length, to such an extent that at times I wondered whether God-talk made any sense. Now I was being addressed by God in a way that simply sidestepped all the questions I had, first through the panhandler's prayer, then through a slick preacher.

I was still trying to deal with the impact of the preacher's words when someone came over to me and asked whether I would be willing to give thanks for the cup at communion. Give thanks for the cup!? By now my spiritual nerves were so sensitive, I was again overcome emotionally, this time by the significance of drinking from the cup with Jesus. How could I know what sharing the cup with Christ would mean for my life? And was I prepared to be thankful for that? The words of the preacher were still fresh in my mind. I did find the courage to thank God, all the while yearning for enough faith to live up the gift of God's call, whatever that might bring.

These experiences represented a crucial turning point, conversion, in my life. In the years since I have still had many questions; I have experienced times of great weakness in my faith and relationships. But I left Ottawa that summer with great joy and peace and some important insights. God had met me in persons and in ways I could never have predicted. That was unsettling, but I have found it to be a great source of hope. God is always ahead of us, perhaps out of sight, ready to surprise us with grace, inviting us, sometimes pulling us into a future where God is already present. There is no need to fear.

In the days and weeks that followed those turbulent days in Ottawa, I began to feel joy, to feel pain, to cry, to love. I began to know what it feels like to love God, and, far more importantly, to live with a constant sense that no matter what, I am known and loved by God. That confidence has never left me. And that makes all the difference in the world. ∎

Tom Yoder Neufeld was born in Winnipeg, Manitoba, Canada, in 1947. He grew up in Europe where his parents were in church work. After college, university, and seminary studies, Tom worked with inner-city poor, as a prison and hospital chaplain, and as a pastor in northern Canada. He presently teaches New Testament at Conrad Grebel

College, a Mennonite college affiliated with the University of Waterloo, Ontario. His wife, Rebecca, is a pastor. They have two pre-teenagers, David and Miriam. Tom loves singing and painting almost as much as teaching and preaching.

14

God, You're Not Supposed to Work Like This Today

J. Lorne Peachey

SAMUEL AND GIDEON. These two biblical characters were boyhood heroes of mine. How I marveled as I heard their stories in my Sunday school classes at Locust Grove Mennonite Church in Belleville, Pennsylvania, in the early 1940s. A direct voice from God for Samuel. A sign for Gideon—not one but two. I envied such direct, intimate communication with the Almighty. Envied, yes. Expected to experience, no.

How did God speak to Samuel? To Gideon? Was it through an audible voice? An inner nudge? Why didn't God speak to me that way?

Not that I asked any of these questions out loud. You didn't in my Sunday school days. Instead, you learned you should to be ready to be obedient to God's call. The "when" and the "how" were things you just somehow knew when the call came, mostly by thinking a lot about it.

These were valuable lessons for me. God is knowable. You use your head. You study, think, pray, and think some more. Then you will understand—and know God. It was a good theology that went well with keeping the fencerows clean, the corn rows straight, and the garden weed free—other values I absorbed during my first eighteen years on a

Kishacoquillas Valley farm.

That sense of knowing God through one's mind, of being able to think and meet God through one's reason, followed me during my years of education—first at Belleville Mennonite School and then at Eastern Mennonite College (now University), Harrisonburg, Virginia. True, I did make two forays into the secular education world—a summer at Penn State University and a year of graduate school at Syracuse (New York) University. But even there, where God was occasionally challenged or even ridiculed, thinking and reasoning came in handy as a defense of a personal God. God could be reasoned. Faith was measurable.

It was a good environment in which to grow up. I came to embrace the faith of my childhood as a personal one that came to sustain, comfort, and lead. My faith was one possible through the intellect.

At the same time, God's ways were at the same time often inscrutable for me. I remembered Samuel and Gideon. No, God apparently didn't speak that way today. But wouldn't it be great if God did?

I remember asking that question often in 1964 when trying to decide if my future was to be in education or journalism. I had spent three good years in the classroom teaching English, journalism, and biology at Western Mennonite School, Salem, Oregon. Then I got a call asking me to consider returning to Pennsylvania to become an editorial assistant at the Mennonite Publishing House, Scottdale, Pennsylvania. How I agonized over that decision. I loved teaching. But I also wanted to edit. Finally, somewhat reluctantly, I chose the latter.

Sometimes I still wonder how my life might have been different had I chosen teaching. Without a direct call or sign about which way to go, I reasoned that likely either way would have been God's will for me. Somehow God finds a way to work with us on the path we choose.

God of the mind. It was a satisfying experience of the divine presence for me. But it began to change in the spring of 1989. The catalyst: a possible call to edit the weekly publication of the Mennonite Church, *Gospel Herald*.

By that time I had already spent twenty years editing publications for the church—first a youth magazine, *With*; later a leisure-reading magazine, *Christian Living*. Then in my mid-forties, I had become restless. I decided I wanted to do something other than church work, which I had been in all my life. So in 1985, when I had an opportunity to become manager of Pennsylvania Mennonite Federal Credit Union, with offices also in Scottdale, I lapped it up as something new.

The job was enjoyable. I liked the challenge. I found finances engrossing. I met new people with new ideas. I began to get involved in the Pennsylvania state credit union movement. I enrolled in several courses to receive my certification as a credit union manager.

Then early in 1989, I became aware that some of my friends had suggested my name to a search committee looking for a new editor for *Gospel Herald*. Of course, I was flattered. But I didn't take it seriously. After all, I had already edited two publications for the church. Certainly I wouldn't be asked to do a third. Surely the church wanted new blood to edit its "official" publication.

By spring I learned I had better take the idea more seriously. The search committee was doing so. But I began to ask questions. Did I really want to get back into church work again? Did I want to exchange something I knew I enjoyed for a task I knew would be difficult? Did I want to give up the relative security of a low-profile job as a credit union manager for what I knew would be a position full of pressures?

All this was boiling in my head on a sunny spring day

while I was driving on the Pennsylvania Turnpike on a business trip for the credit union. I was mulling over these questions as I pulled into the South Somerset Plaza for a break. I can still go to the spot where it happened—second parking space to the left of the front door. As I opened the car door to step out, I heard a voice that said, "Lorne, what would it take to convince you that you should edit *Gospel Herald?*"

Audible or not, I don't know. I did know then—and know now—that it was God's voice. And even before I took another step, I also knew the answers. There were two. One had to do with how much I'd be paid. The other was whether or not I could work with computers.

Petty answers, really! So petty that not until I was driving again did I finally admit them even to myself.

Of course, I didn't share that experience with anyone. Not with such small embarrassing conditions. Besides, you don't talk wages with other people. And you certainly don't hinge a major career decision, let alone a call from the church, on whether or not you get to use a computer—something I had learned to do and enjoy in my role as a credit union manager. So I was mum. I almost forgot about the incident.

Some three months later, J. Robert Ramer, head of Mennonite Publishing House, invited me to lunch. We had become good friends and occasionally spent our lunch hour talking about his work with the church or mine with the credit union. On this day Bob wanted to talk about what it might be like if I got the invitation to join the MPH staff as *Gospel Herald* editor. I didn't say much. I didn't have the courage to tell my friend Bob that I wasn't sure I'd accept if asked.

We finished lunch and began to drive the ten miles back to our offices. We had just crossed a bridge over the turnpike when Bob said suddenly, "Oh, I almost forgot.

I've been checking into salaries. If you do join us, I think your salary should be—" The figure he quoted was the same, to the penny, as the one I knew I wanted three months back at the South Somerset Plaza.

I said nothing. Silence. Bob seemed not to notice. "And there's something else," he continued. "I've noticed how much you enjoy working with computers in the credit union. I think it's time to computerize the *Gospel Herald* office. I want you to do this for us if you're the next editor."

Stunned, I said almost nothing the rest of the way home. I excused myself early from the office, went home, and climbed on my bicycle. Cycling up and down the hills of western Pennsylvania, I kept saying over and over, "God, you're not supposed to work like this today. Voices are what happened to Samuel. Signs are what you gave Gideon. I never asked for a voice. I never begged for a sign. And I got both. Two signs, in fact!"

At least I took them as signs. What's more important, from that day I began to experience God in a new way. Where once I had found God through reasoning, now I was coming to know God through experience—through a voice, through signs, even through physical feelings.

There was the day several months after I had been asked to edit *Gospel Herald*—and had said yes—that I faced a tough, heart-wrenching decision. I left the office and headed for Laurelville Mennonite Church Center to walk the mountain trails. Just after I went under a turnpike overpass (there was that turnpike again!), I felt as though someone had put arms around me. It was a literal, physical warmth. I knew it was God's Spirit. I knew I was not alone. I knew I had the help I needed for the decision I had to make.

Another time there was a day things were clicking just right. A well-written manuscript arrived in the mail that complimented perfectly one I already had on hand. We received several news stories on the same theme as features I had scheduled months earlier for that week's issue of *Gospel Herald.*

I don't know why everything's working so well, I remember thinking. *It has to be the Spirit.*

Just a few minutes later my assistant came into the office. "Why are things going so well?" she asked. "It must be the Spirit!"

It was the Spirit. It is the Spirit. For me, that is an incredible gift from God. The faith I have today has come through nothing I have done or anything I am. It is simply a gift. Grace. All I have needed to do is be open and respond when God comes.

And marvel at how God works. In my first fifty years, God gave me faith through my ability to think and reason. More recently faith has come through direct, personal encounters. I firmly believe there will be greater and different experiences of God's presence for me in the future.

Then there's heaven. The ultimate experience of God's presence. When I arrive, I'll be looking up Samuel and Gideon. What stories we'll have to tell each other. I can hardly wait!   ■

J. Lorne Peachey, Scottdale, Pennsylvania, has been editor of *Gospel Herald,* the weekly publication of the Mennonite Church, since 1990. Lorne and his wife, Emily, are the parents of two grown children, Jon and Anita. They are members of Kingview Mennonite Church. In addition to his work as editor and credit union manager, Lorne has also served on the Coordinating Council of Allegheny Mennonite Conference and as a member of the Mennonite Board of Congregational Ministries.

15

Converted—Again and Again

Doug Pritchard

I WAS thirty-one and living in Australia when I first encountered Jesus. It was there—as my wife, Jane, and I were expecting the birth of our first child, while I was far away from familiar culture, friends, and family—that I had a spiritual awakening.

I asked myself, "What will I teach this child and why? Will I just teach him to be nice because being nice is nicer than not being nice? Or is there something more lasting I can pass on with integrity?" I had been sent to a local United Church Sunday school during my childhood in northern Ontario. I remembered the church had claimed to have lasting truths. So Jane and I went church shopping. We wound up in an evangelical Anglican church because people were friendly, and there were lots of other babies in baskets on the back pew.

With great reluctance I also joined one of the church's Bible study groups. I was quickly confronted with the person of Christ. Was he really the Son of God? Did that matter? The study was led by a young minister who had been a historian and government archivist before entering the ministry. So the historical accuracy of the Bible was crucial to him—and me.

After a few months of study, I accepted that the Christian faith did make sense intellectually—God sent an only

Son to earth to show us God's way and to die in our place; all who repent and believe this are saved. I accepted Jesus as my Savior in my mind. Was that enough?

Jane and I had itchy feet and wanted to travel again. I made some halfhearted inquiries into mission work. Fortunately most agencies immediately said no. I was relieved. It wasn't "the Lord's will"! Then the Australian chemical firm for which I worked offered me the big new job in Germany which I had lusted after for ages. I rushed home to tell Jane the good news that we were moving to Munich in six weeks. I never bothered to ask whether she could work in Germany or wanted to move there.

That same week we were offered a term of Voluntary Service in Bangladesh with Mennonite Central Committee. Suddenly I had a dramatic choice to make between the job I had wanted so much in this life and the unknown of a Voluntary Service assignment. I knew it was a choice for which I would be accountable eternally. I knew that one day I would stand before the judgment seat of God and give an account of my choice on this day. Jesus wanted me to follow him in more than just my mind. Accepting the Bangladesh assignment was the first time I put my life in Jesus' hands and was born-again a citizen of his kingdom. In so doing I found peace with God.

The time in Bangladesh changed my life. Seeing up close the suffering caused by the greed and fear in the world meant I could no longer ignore my own complicity in such pain and my duty to the poor.

The healthcare project where we worked was next to an army base. I remember how well fed and well dressed the soldiers were. They sat under shade trees and did blackboard drills while nearby starving women with nursing infants broke bricks under a searing sun. Bangladesh's independence was won by violence; and soldiers, police, and bandits perpetuate the cycle of violence and death.

Later, back in Australia, I had trouble making sense of this. Mennonites I met in Bangladesh had explained to me some of the historic basis for Christian opposition to the use of violence. Then a friend invited Jane and me to a weekend conference organized by an ecumenical group called the Churches Working Group for Peace. I heard there a clear account of the Bible's teaching on peace.

I heard also the stories of Christian peacemakers who had tried to live out that teaching. I heard of a Catholic priest imprisoned in the Philippines for his work with the oppressed; a Baptist pastor threatened with death for assisting refugees in Australia; an aristocratic Anglican lawyer ostracized for his outspoken opposition to nuclear weapons. I was powerfully moved by this teaching and testimony. That weekend I became a convert to Jesus' way of peace.

Jane and I began to work at peace issues in our church and community. But it was much harder to work at peace in our own home. A serious conflict arose between us when we returned to Canada three years later. I was working long hours managing a chemical plant in Toronto, Ontario. Jane began to work part-time in family medicine after a break of seven years. Our boys were ages nine, seven, and three. So we started the frenzied round of babysitters, daycare, and hurried meals common to many households today.

Jane was soon offered a chance for some special training and a full-time job. She was delighted. I was dismayed. I feared more childcare problems, more chaotic housekeeping, and . . . more constraints on how I pursued my own career. I said no, impossible, it can't work. She was furious. And rightly so. I was trying to control her.

At the same time, as I looked ahead, I found it harder and harder to make any personal plans. At work I made all sorts of plans—yearly budgets, five-year plans, ten-year plans. But I couldn't do the same for myself. Deep within I knew there was a basic conflict between where I was going and where I should be going. I knew that my life's priorities should be God first, family second, work third. Yet I had put them in the reverse order—work first, then family, then God. My conflict with Jane reflected this. It was also a matter of domestic justice. Why should my job come first?

I was challenged and encouraged by a number of men friends who, by choice or by layoff, were at home with their children while their wives worked outside. The men often found this change painful. I was haunted by one friend whose right arm became paralyzed for a while after he left work. He told me that arm had been his "power arm"—the one with which he signed checks, answered the phone, greeted visitors—and now he had cut it off to be home with his children. I caught a glimpse of how a woman might feel when a child invades her womb and cuts off a career. I am grateful to Jane and other women and men who helped me see that childcare is also a part of living peacefully and seeking justice.

After months of struggle, I finally let go of my need for approval from bosses, peers, and parents; left my paid job; and took on the main parenting role at home. It was a scary time for me, but it has been exciting to see Jane grow in her self-confidence and sense of fulfillment in her own ministry among refugees and the disadvantaged in our city. It has been exciting to get to know my boys better and to offer them a more complete model of parenting than I did before. My situation has also given me an opportunity to work on peace and justice issues in my own Mennonite church conference as a part-time volunteer.

Despite my conversion to Christ, to peace, to justice, there are many parts of my life I am struggling to give over to God. Our family is still far more privileged than most of the world's people. I am troubled by the racism I still find surfacing from deep within me.

I also see more clearly the evil grasp militarism has on our society. Our children are exposed to it in school trips to military forts, in violent films, and when offered learning opportunities in weapons plants. But I am encouraged that their schools are introducing "Peacemaker" programs for conflict resolution. Our friends struggle with militarism when asked to work on military contracts by their employers. But I am encouraged by those who make life-affirming career choices, even in the midst of a recession.

I face militarism every April when asked to pay taxes to support an ever growing military budget despite the hungry and homeless on our streets. I can no longer pay taxes to support the military. I redirect the military portion of my federal income taxes to the peace tax fund administered by Conscience Canada, despite the objections of Revenue Canada.

The struggle with "the cosmic powers of this present darkness" is a real one. But my path is lit by Jesus, the true light, who came into the world that we might have life and have it abundantly. The Bible assures me Jesus himself is our peace, who has made the two one and destroyed the dividing wall of hostility between men and women, between Jew and Samaritan, between us and God. In Christ, I have peace with God; in Christ, I have the peace of God; in Christ, I receive power to make peace in this world. ■

Doug Pritchard and his wife, Jane, are parents of two teenagers, David and Michael, and of a near-teenager, Paul. They are members of Toronto United Mennonite Church in Toronto, Ontario. Doug is a chemical engineer by training and now serves as peace, justice, and social concerns coordinator for the Mennonite Conference of Eastern Canada. He also sings in Pax Christi Chorale and makes great spaghetti sauce.

16

Grace, Revival Fires and an Anabaptist Pilgrimage

John D. Roth

CHILDREN growing up in religious homes have much for which to be thankful. But the warm, nurturing context of childhood faith—especially in Mennonite households—can also create a certain confusion about the nature of sin and our corresponding need for God's grace.

Like many other young Mennonites, I grew up in a fairly traditional, stable, two-parent Christian family. At our home we regularly paused for devotions, prayed at mealtime (even in restaurants!), and could be found in church every Sunday morning, Sunday evening, and Wednesday evening. In my childhood, Christian identity was embedded in a culture which permeated all of life, affecting not only the nature of our work and our entertainment, but also the way we dressed, spoke, behaved, and thought.

In virtually all respects it was a good childhood, filled with structure, security, and love. But at the same time, I also recall hearing sermons which stressed the significance of choice in matters of faith. Unlike our Lutheran or Catholic neighbors, we Mennonites believed in the idea of adult, or believers, baptism. Children were not simply born into the church; rather each individual chose to enter the church of his or her own free will.

Many of the sermons, echoing the rugged dualism of

the Schleitheim Confession, made it clear that there were only two options in this world: the kingdom of darkness or the kingdom of light, a life of sin and wickedness or a life of redemption. There was no middle ground between the fellowship of adult believers and the fallen world all around. This point was reinforced in those occasional Sunday evening services when ex-junkies and former gang members from places like Chicago and New York City told harrowing tales of conversion from wickedness and crime to the peace of Jesus Christ.

All this served to complicate the picture. I would lie in bed at night pondering the mysteries of urban evil, reflecting on the kingdom of darkness and the kingdom of light, and wondering where I, a conscientious, morally scrupulous, somewhat nerdy, nine-year-old boy fitted in. I was not yet a baptized member of the church. Therefore I must still be in the kingdom of darkness. But up against the likes of a Nicky Cruz, it somehow seemed my life of sin failed to qualify. How do children nurtured in Christian homes, raised in the family of God, cross the great divide and become adult members of the church?

My solution, as it turned out, came in the spring of 1969. One Sunday morning an announcement was made in church that Holmes County (Ohio) was—spiritually speaking—a "field white unto harvest." An evangelist well known in Mennonite circles had consented to come to the area to begin the task of winnowing and reaping. The meetings were originally scheduled to last one week. Since this was a relatively unusual happening, it was simply assumed that our family—all five children—would attend each night of the revival.

I vividly recall the electricity in the air that first Sunday evening as we drove toward Berlin and saw the tent looming on the horizon in the pasture field at Sturgis Miller's farm. There were men scurrying about with flashlights and special red canes as they parked the cars which were converging in long lines off State Road 39. I remember the walk through the pasture to the enormous tent, along with hundreds of people—all freshly scrubbed—streaming in from all sides. There inside the tent amidst the smell of fresh sawdust were hundreds of wooden folding chairs and special hymnbooks. At the front, a flatbed trailer doubled as a stage.

I shivered with excitement as the singing began. Then I was completely engulfed in the booming voice of the evangelist who, in simple, vivid terms, outlined the steps of salvation. "The wages of sin is death, but the gift of God is eternal life." There it was in a nutshell: all of us were destined to a life in eternity; the question was only whether that life in eternity was going to be in heaven or the fiery pits of hell.

Then, almost without warning, it came—the fateful moment of decision, the invitation to come forward and to make a public declaration of commitment to Christ. That first Sunday evening, I was so transfixed by the surroundings, so awed by the drama of the event itself (this was, after all, in the days before TV was common in Holmes County Mennonite households) that I was simply too paralyzed even to consider going forward.

But Monday was a long day. Never before was I so keenly aware of the wages of sin; never before had I thought so much about the nature of fire; never before had I been so grateful for the gift of God's forgiving grace. On Monday night, almost as soon as the invitation was extended—the choir wasn't even through the first verse of "Just As I Am"—I took that long walk forward, met my prayer partner, and said a prayer of confession.

Now things would have been fine if the revival team, having successfully seen me into the fold, had folded the tent, and moved on. Unfortunately, however, we were still early in the week. On Tuesday night the invitation was extended to those who had once made a commitment but might now want to *rededicate* their lives to Jesus. After only a moment of reflection, I decided that probably applied to me. So I lurched off down the aisle once again.

On Wednesday night I had resolved—thanks to the good counsel of my parents—to resist any urge I might have to go forward. But just as things were winding up, the evangelist told a long and complicated story—a story about a man who had made and then squandered a fortune—which put things in a completely new perspective. The story was haunting and compelling. And when the preacher suddenly said, "Young man, is the Lord calling you?" I was certain he was pointing directly at me, and it seemed like the right thing to do.

By Thursday evening, I was on a first-name basis with the prayer partners up front. Haunted by the thought of eternity and convinced there were still sins in my young life which had not yet been rooted out, when the call came for "backsliders," I knew this category too included me.

And I wasn't the only one. Indeed, by the end of the week, the success of the revival meeting had been so great that community leaders decided to continue it for yet another week. I remember crying all the way home on hearing that news, wondering if I could handle another week of soul searching.

I am aware that Christians of goodwill have differed on the place of revival meetings. Many Mennonites who came of age in the revival era like to criticize such meetings for their emotional manipulation or theological naïveté. And there was a period in my own life when I tried to reject completely that experience, fancying that the emotional trauma I had endured during revival was the source of everything that might have gone wrong in my spiritual life thereafter.

But today I'm not so sure. As I now reflect on the event, it strikes me that the experience at the revival meetings shaped my faith in the years that followed in several significant ways. For one thing, long after the meetings were over, the event helped remind me that in matters of faith there is indeed a battle. Even without the vivid imagery of angels and demons, the fiery pit of hell, or the tranquil bliss of heaven, I know today with the evangelist that there is such a thing as evil in the world. I affirm that evil takes a surprising variety of expressions, and that as Christians we are called to name the evils and to move forward confidently in the strength of God.

The event also reminds me that faith does imply an active choice with a public dimension. It is often easy for those raised in the church to forget that being part of the family of God is not the same thing as making a decision to join the church of Jesus Christ. Whatever reservations one might have about the approach, revival meetings provided an important opportunity for young people nurtured in Christian homes to make public decisions.

Even more importantly, I affirm the language of grace which imbued those sermons in the revival tent. To be sure, talk about God's grace can be become trite, formulaic, cheap. But the Christianity of my youth was defined almost exclusively in terms of good works or proper behavior. If nothing else, the language of the revival was a reminder that no amount of good deeds, discipleship training, Voluntary Service, Mennonite Disaster Service, or Mennonite Central Committee assignments—all excellent activities—are a substitute in the end for the free gift of God's forgiveness and grace.

A full decade after my experience at the revival meetings, a sequel to the story occurred which offered further testimony to the surprising ways God's grace can be revealed. Intent on getting an education, I had just completed a year in college. I had traveled a long way since my earnest, innocent days in the spring of 1969. I had discovered, at the ripe age of eighteen, that the mark of a truly educated person was systematic doubt. I had long since begun to doubt the wisdom of my parents; I was beginning to entertain doubts about my faith; and after a brief encounter with the college classroom, I also had begun to doubt the educational system itself. At some point I reached the decision that to get properly educated, I would have to do it on my own.

So I left college to see the world. Through a fortunate set of connections, I came in contact with a family in Austria and made arrangements to live and work on their small farm. In October, following the harvest season, the family offered to buy me a three-week train ticket to travel anywhere in Europe. So I set about to make travel plans.

I was determined from the outset not to turn my vacation into a Mennonite pilgrimage to the Anabaptist "holy lands." Instead, I eyed the country which seemed to offer the greatest contrast to the world of Mennonites, both geographically and spiritually—Greece.

In Greece, far from home, far from the Mennonite work ethic, I could relax on the beaches, enjoying the clear sky and the warm breezes blowing in off the deep blue Aegean Sea. In contrast to my own provincial past, I reasoned, Greece was a land of real culture, the home of Plato and Socrates, Aristotle and Aristophanes, Aeschylus and Euripides. Here at the wellsprings of an ancient and pagan culture, amidst the ruins of the Acropolis, I could ponder the meaning of life.

The only problem was money. I had a rail ticket with unlimited miles, but I was resigned to living on a tight budget for food and accommodations.

I arrived in Greece late on a Saturday night and woke up early the next Sunday morning eager to stroll through

Athens, to take in the sights, and to get a feel for the lay of the land. It was a wonderful day.

But late in the afternoon, as I was walking back to the youth hostel, an agitated young man approached me. In broken German he told me his story. He was a Yugoslavian, in Greece only for the weekend to gamble with some friends. Fortune, he claimed, had smiled on him. He had won thousands of Greek drachmas; but the banks were closed and drachmas were hard to exchange in Yugoslavia. After some hurried negotiating, we finally agreed to a black-market exchange at double the official rate.

At the end of the transaction, he handed me a thick wad of bills and left with my Austrian schillings as I carefully stuffed his drachmas into a neck purse for safekeeping. As I continued on my way, I could only marvel at my good fortune. I had only been in Greece a single day, and already things were going great. Thoughts of skiing at Saint Moritz flitted at the edge of my mind.

When I got back to my room to count the money again, however, those thoughts, along with all my plans, came to crashing end. I did not have 8000 drachmas but a single drachma note, wrapped neatly around a wad of Italian newspaper carefully cut to size. It was a shattering moment. I was angry and humiliated. Visions of strolling leisurely through the Acropolis, of lolling on Greek beaches, suddenly evaporated. Moreover, I still had a full two weeks of travel ahead of me, now with a budget of $30.

The next morning I took the first train to Europe I could find to the mainland. I had no clear sense of destination or purpose. I just wanted to get out of Athens. For a whole day, then most of the night, I sat immobile in the northbound train, alternately cursing my own stupidity and humanity in general. Toward morning, I remember waking up and hearing the conductor announce the next stop as Zurich, Switzerland.

Without really intending to, I stumbled off the train, backpack in tow, and began to wander around the city. Eventually I came to the Limmat River and followed along its banks until I arrived at a large cathedral, the Grossmünster church, with a large statue of Ulrich Zwingli, the famous Swiss Reformer, prominently displayed outside. I walked inside the church and slipped into a pew, tired, angry, nearly in tears.

As I sat there I slowly became aware of English-speaking voices. Another American tour group, I snarled inwardly. But there was something distinctive about one particular voice that suddenly caught my attention. In an instant it became clear to me. The booming voice belonged to none other than revivalist George R. Brunk II, my erstwhile friend and tormentor of a decade or so earlier. With him was a Mennonite tour group *freundschaft*—my father's second cousins from West Liberty, Ohio; a close friend of my uncles' from Archbold, Ohio; and a bunch of Lederachs and Yoders I didn't know at all, but it didn't matter! There they were, salt-of-the-earth retirees, farmers, carpenters, millworkers. Not a Greek philosopher in the group. But they were my people. They fed me, welcomed me for a night, took up a small collection on my behalf, and sent me on my way.

I left Zurich a changed person. I had not found my people; rather, my people had found me. I had been embraced by a community of God's people. And in that moment, I knew I had been touched by the grace of God. ∎

John D. Roth grew up in Holmes County, Ohio. Currently he is associate professor of history at Goshen (Indiana) College where, in addition to teaching, he serves as director of the Mennonite Historical Library and editor of *The Mennonite Quarterly Review*. He and his wife, Ruth, are parents of four daughters and are active in the Berkey Avenue Mennonite Fellowship.

17

People on a Bus: Some Confessions

Gerald W. Schlabach

EIGHT YEARS AGO I was traveling by bus from my home in Honduras to meetings in neighboring Guatemala. The meetings were part of my assignment to develop and coordinate Mennonite Central Committee (MCC) work for peace and justice in Central America. Of all the projects this work involved, my passion was to write a short book on the biblical basis of Christian service. Mennonites have served other communities around the world but have written surprisingly little on the subject. We now felt the lack of theological resources sharply.

I had gotten to the bus station in plenty of time to get a seat. It would be a long, tiring day. But at least it gave me a chance to read a book I had been wanting to read—as long as I had a seat. And now I did have a seat.

As the bus traveled, it picked up additional passengers. I kept my nose in my book. The aisle eventually filled. I kept my nose in my book, reading something that would help me write about Mennonite servanthood. I realized that the peasant woman standing next to me was pregnant.

I kept my seat.

I realized I was being selfish. I kept my seat.

At some level, deep inside, I realized I was sinning against everything I believed in, everything I was teaching and writing about, everything I thought I was in Central

America to do. Still I kept my seat.

I saw the ugliness in my heart, the hidden sin that is all the more vicious because it wears a cloak of respectability.

I am a sinner.

* * *

It didn't help that the book I was reading was Reinhold Niebuhr's classic challenge to Christian pacifists and liberal do-gooders, *Moral Man and Immoral Society*. Writing in the 1930s, Niebuhr ruthlessly exposed the selfishness of human beings and the communities in which they live. People may be capable of self-giving love in their face-to-face relationships, in families, in local communities. But even when they selflessly seek the good of some they inevitably slight others. Further, he argued, groups are even less capable of putting aside their self-interest than individuals.

I was preparing to argue back. God's intention in calling out a people was to leaven human history with a social group that is an exception to Niebuhr's rule. God had blessed Abraham and Sarah, not so they could hoard God's blessings, so that they might be a blessing to all peoples. When God's people fail in this calling, God re-empowers them by standing in their place as the suffering servant Jesus Christ, by raising them up in the Holy Spirit. Instead, there I sat.

Yet in the end, it *did* help that the book I was reading was Niebuhr's. For years, that pregnant peasant woman quietly haunted my memory. Niebuhr would not let me forget her. The two of them would not let me deceive myself or evade my God.

Rarely, however, do people recognize the turning points in their lives immediately. I kept thinking and writing about "theology of service." MCC asked me to write a book encouraging Christians to relate and respond to the poor. "We don't want one more guilt trip," came the instructions. "We don't need one more issues piece, heavy on social and political analysis. Find a different approach, one that will motivate people in any Sunday school classroom. Don't preach simply to the 'converted' social activists."

The assignment took me back to basics. What really motivates people to care about others? What motivates people to respond to the poor? What motivates people to expose themselves to the suffering of others in the first place, encountering others not just as social issues, but as human beings?

The assignment took me back to myself as well. My editor kept prodding me. A deeply spiritual African-American, John was quick to note ways that well-intentioned North American Christians relate to the poor from positions of strength—while hiding their own neediness, their own poverty. He was right. Even when I forgot about the peasant woman, I could not forget that my wife and I had come back from five years in Central America burned out, tired, depressed, and a lot less idealistic. I was needy too.

Yet so much of my theology was about discipleship, following Jesus, servanthood. Not only was my job to keep writing about such things, but the ability of people like Mennonites to respond to the challenge of people like Niebuhr seems to require *proving* that the Christian community can do better than the norm.

And in the eyes of many, Mennonites do. We have won recognition around the world for the quiet integrity (and low financial overhead) with which we work at grassroots community development, provide relief in disaster situations that television crews ignore or soon forget, and work to change unjust conflict situations while respecting the human dignity of all parties.

If proving something is *why* we serve, however, Niebuhr would be right to call the effort one more example of self-centered human action. This time they just happen to wear good deeds as a disguise! If this is *why* we serve, Martin Luther before him would have been right to call it "justification by works." Even those of us who have stopped striving anxiously to earn our salvation before God may anxiously continue to demonstrate our moral integrity before women and men.

If so we are doing exactly what Luther warned against in his penetrating treatise *On the Freedom of a Christian*. We are using the needy "neighbor" to meet our need to prove our goodness, rather than freely serving the neighbor with a love like that of Christ's love for us.

The last thing I wanted to do when I wrote *And Who Is My Neighbor?* and *To Bless All Peoples*, however, was to sound like Luther. "Justification by faith alone" would undermine the call for discipleship and Christian service, wouldn't it? The more theologians like Luther or Augustine before him emphasized God's grace, the more they seemed to lower the standards of Christian ethics. Long after I finished writing these books, that bothered me. When I finally had to answer two questions, "Why care about the poor?" and "Why serve others?" my answers sounded so Lutheran.

A few years later I would read Augustine and Luther for myself, fighting hard.

They won.

Oh, not on every point, of course. I still question the alliances they made with the state, their law-and-order approaches to social justice, and their rationalizations for Christians using violence. But now I question such judgments on the basis of shared convictions about the identify of Jesus Christ, the triune life of God, and above all the absolute need of human beings for God's grace.

I am now convinced that far from undermining Mennonite faithfulness to Jesus' teachings of nonviolent love of neighbor, we can only be faithful insofar as we act in grateful, trusting faith in Jesus Christ. When Jesus of Nazareth was faithful even to death on the cross, God in Christ did all that is needed to save and empower us.

* * *

I doubt that my story is unique. I suspect others are on this same bus ride.

This story does not have to begin with Augustine's restless inner scrutiny or with Luther's quest for release from a guilty conscience. In many Christian churches, including Mennonite ones, the main problem is not how to answer a supposedly harsh, demanding, and just God, but this: what will the community think, how will we look the bishop or Aunt Matilda in the eye? What if Grandpa finds out we go to movies or drink beer?

Such is life in what anthropologists might call a "shame culture" rather than a "guilt culture." Yet we need forgiveness no less! Tight-knit communities can be harder on their members than "God the Father" himself.

This sense of failure is not simply an individual matter. A sense of peoplehood, of community, may in fact sharpen it. As Mennonites in North America during the last few generations have quickly joined the mainstream culture, we have sometimes mourned our failure to maintain a distinct identity. Meanwhile new tugs and callings have pulled in various directions. Some worry that we are not being faithful at evangelizing. Some worry that we are not in consistent solidarity with the oppressed. Some worry that we are losing our peace witness. Some have set up ten-year goals for church planting and missions. Some have founded peacemaker teams.

Legitimate worries. Worthy goals.

But God help us!

God help us—because if faithfulness depends on *our* doing, we're sunk. We dig ourselves deeper, we sap the spiritual resources that do remain in our community, when we try to do it on our own. Mennonite evangelicals and Mennonite activists have the same problem—our "oughts." We ought to evangelize, ought to care about the poor, ought to bring our taxable income down so we're not part of the war machine. All worthy concerns—none that I want to give up. Yet our only hope of faithfulness is the faithfulness of Jesus Christ at work in our midst.

There may be no more adequate way to sum up why we so desperately need grace than to follow Luther's lead one more time by drawing on his robust use of earthy talk: We just keep defecating on each other with our "oughts."

In doing so, we bury the hope and trust in God that animate joyful witnessing *and* joyful identification with the needy. An ethic purely of discipleship will leave us burned out—whether as social activists or faithful Sunday school teachers or evangelists. In fact, it may drive us *away* from following Christ. Mennonite writers have often quoted the Anabaptist Hans Denck: "No one can know Christ unless they follow him in life." But Denck added, "and no one can follow Christ unless they know him."

* * *

To leave matters there, however, merely adds one more "ought"—Mennonites ought to trust in God's grace, ought to experience God's grace. The dilemma for revivalists and theologians alike is that precisely because grace is God's doing, we cannot program it. At most we proclaim it, confess it, and thus make a space for it by acknowledging our own emptiness.

Perhaps the fact that I continue spending much time with books remains something to confess! At least I can confess with certainty that God has had the grace to meet me even there. In forcing me back to the basics of Christian faith, God has used the theologians I once found threatening to rebuild my commitment to nonviolence and servanthood on the foundation of grace.

After agreeing with so much of what Augustine said about our need for grace, what Luther said about our need for trusting faith in Christ alone, and what Niebuhr said about the human condition that makes it so—why, unlike all three, am I still a pacifist? Why, in other words, do I continue to believe it is possible for the Christian community to live for other communities in a way that precludes violence and witnesses to Christ's love?

Ultimately there is only one reason. It is the reason that makes all other reasons possible. It goes something like this: *Jesus loves me, this I know, for the Bible tells me so. Little ones to him belong. They are weak but he is strong.*

That is not the only reason I am a pacifist, but it is the first, last, and best reason. Jesus loves me, loves us. The biblical story tells us just how great is that love.

We were God's enemies, lost in sin, lost in our own self-worship, lost in rebellion, but God—whom we had made our enemy—took the initiative! This is the message of Romans 5, for example. In Jesus Christ, *God* took the way of the cross, the way of peaceable servanthood, and God did it *first*! God's action in Jesus Christ is the beginning. If God's love was so great that God could love you and me while we were yet sinners, then God's love can empower us to love others while they are yet sinners. If that healing, reconciling love grips us to the core, how else can we respond except by loving our own enemies, even if they do us harm?

"We love because he first loved us." That is how 1 John

4:19 puts it. But we find the pattern throughout the Bible. Even in the Law of Moses, God's gracious act comes first. We respond in kind, not because God is harsh and fickle and might strike us down. We respond lovingly because God loves us first, and the only appropriate response is to love others in the same way.

Remember the parable of the ungrateful servant? Jesus once told of a king who canceled a million-dollar debt and of a debtor who refused to cancel the debt of a fellow servant. The king's overwhelming, ridiculously generous forgiveness begged for a like response. Couldn't the servant have forgiven his fellow servant's measly debt? The pattern is the same. We love because God first loves us.

Or take the classic text in Matthew 5 says, "Love your enemies and pray for those who persecute you." Why? Because that is the way our heavenly Parent is! God makes the rain fall on the just and the unjust. God loves without discrimination. God loves God's enemies. We see it in the rain. We see it on the cross. The pattern is the same.

If the first step in the life of grace and graciousness is one that *we* must take, or if we travel this path through our own power once we are on it, *then the cross will grind us into dust.* Anyone with a sensitive conscience may despair. Those already in subservient roles may think it sinful even to care about their own welfare, much less demand respect for their rights. Unless we are clear about this, the cross may become a sign of grinding oppression for all who were raised on stories of self-sacrifice and service rather than the sign and power of God's love.

Too often this is what has happened in our church. When we stress that the essence of Christianity is discipleship—following Jesus—everything seems to begin when we hear the words of Jesus, "if anyone would follow me, take up your cross daily. For whoever saves their live will lose it, and whoever loses their life will save it. The greatest in the kingdom is the servant of all" (author's paraphrase).

But look closely. When Jesus said, "Blessed are the merciful," or taught us to forgive, or called his would-be followers to take up their crosses, to whom was he talking? To people who already had sensed a new dignity in his love. To people who already had felt his healing touch. To people already drawn to his life-giving magnetism, his love, his person.

Good news came first. Life came first. Jesus Christ, God's loving *Yes* to us, *came first.*

Why serve others? Why be pacifists? Why love our enemies? Because God is like that. This is our God. This is our salvation. To respond in any other way is to say that we have some other heavenly parent, another god. To respond in any other way is to make light of our salvation, to be ungrateful.

Yet I confess that I have been ungrateful. I confess that we do respond in other ways. I confess that we sometimes make our theology of peace, justice, and servanthood a substitute for being peaceable, just, loving servants of others.

Grace, gratitude, graciousness. To move us through one to the other is God's doing. Even to confess our sins depends on God's grace. Yet in confessing that, we confess more than our sins. We confess Jesus Christ himself, our only hope. Confession, in fact, ultimately has very little to do with our sin. The real stuff of confession is praise to God.

"Lord, . . . why then do I set out in order before you this account of so many deeds? In truth, it is not that you may learn to know these matters from me, but that I may rouse up towards you my own affections, and those of others who read this, so that all of us may say: "The Lord is great, and exceedingly to be praised."

Augustine, *Confessions* 11.1. ■

Gerald W. Schlabach worked with Mennonite Central Committee (MCC) during most of the 1980s. While in Nicaragua and Honduras, he developed a regional Peace Portfolio for MCC. Since returning to North America he has authored *And Who Is My Neighbor?* (Herald Press, 1990) and *To Bless All Peoples* (Herald Press, 1991). He is completing a doctoral degree in theology and ethics at the University of Notre Dame. He and his wife, Joetta Handrich, are members of Kern Road Mennonite Church in South Bend, Indiana. They have two sons, Gabriel and Jacob.

18

Where Love Is Lodged

Sara Wenger Shenk

I DON'T KNOW where I developed my bent toward skepticism. I teeter continually on the edge of unbelief. Whenever someone sounds too cocksure or glib about how Jesus did this or that for them, I want to needle them with nasty questions to find how deep their confidence goes and whether or not it has been tested by fire.

I like Nathanael. When he hears his brother Philip gushing about how they've found the one foretold by Moses and the prophets, he isn't easily taken in. "Can anything good come out of Nazareth?" he wonders doubtfully. He is, as Jesus perceives, "an Israelite in whom there is no deceit" (John 1:43-46).

I've seen too much religiosity that feels like playacting, where people have the cues down pat but don't remember what the drama is about. I've heard people talk as if God is in their corner and behaves according to the script that they've written. I fume. And I cry. How dare we speak of God except in hushed tones of trembling awe? How dare we let the charade go on, maintaining a form of godliness, but denying its power to blow all our tidy assumptions to smithereens?

Why am I gripped by this prophet's rage, I wonder? What fuels it? Perhaps it's because I also learned well to play the part. I learned early to project the image of confidence—an aura of being more than I really felt I was inside. As a missionary kid sent away to boarding school at six years of age, I learned to excel at being a little adult and pleasing elders. Whether it was keeping a clean room so we'd win the room score competition, learning memory verses so my hand wouldn't be smacked with a ruler, or getting straight As, it all added up to the appearance of being a good, smart, together kid.

I managed fairly well to be what others wanted me to be. When I left boarding school, I received their award for all-round excellence. Then we returned to the States, where our missionary family was put on a heroic pedestal. We were paraded from church to church for display. Everyone seemed to know my father and consequently me too.

I both enjoyed and resented the distinction of my inherited fame. The more others seemed to think of me, the less I thought of myself. Fear stalked my gut. I knew inside that I wasn't what others thought I was. I began a tense vigil over my image, maintaining it despite the fracturing of my inner confidence. The gap between what others thought I was and what I knew I was grew larger with time. It was hard to let people come close to me because I feared that when they discovered I wasn't what I seemed, they would reject me.

A fragile thread of faith wound its way through the fractures. I had dutifully learned the catechism and been baptized at an expected age. I towed the line on hair and dress requirements as stipulated by my church community. I heard endless debates on passages of Scripture related to nonconformity to the world. I knew lines were drawn and distinctions made on the basis of behavior, dictated by a stern authority somewhere.

Up to a point, I fitted in well because I knew how to play by the rules. But somewhere along the way, melancholy, resentment, and cynicism set in. What were the rules for? What end did they serve? Where was the heart in all this legalism and heavy-handed indoctrination?

I didn't know for what I longed, but my longing and loneliness grew ever more acute. Intellectually I knew my denomination had a strong argument for its calling as a countercultural force in our messed-up world. I wanted to remain in my church family, but I had no sense of conviction or passion other than finding fault with its excesses and inconsistencies.

Then love entered the picture. Oh, it had been there all along, in my mother's warm embrace and my father's warbling whistle, but it hadn't drawn me toward God or the church. Now it sidled up and caught my attention. I was a sophomore at a strange new college. We were assigned to read Thomas Merton's *New Seeds of Contemplation* (Abbey of Gethsemane, Inc. 1961) for a creative writing class. I was thoroughly captivated by this man's spiritual insights. Finally someone was speaking to my heart and not just to my head.

I came across an image that so aptly described me that it changed me for life. It described the way I wrapped experience, knowledge, and honor around myself like bandages to make myself visible. But underneath the wrappings, there was no substance. Inside the false self I'd been projecting, I was hollow. And when the wrappings were removed, there was nothing left but my own nakedness and emptiness.

As I read, the Spirit tenderly entered where I was cowering down behind my defenses, unnamed, unclaimed, and homeless; housed, yes, but behind a facade. In those moments, as Merton and the Spirit ministered to me, I began to know love—not love for a dogma or a code of ethics, but for a person, Jesus Christ. It was such a relief to be real with someone and to know I was loved no matter how timid I felt about meeting my own and others' expectations. On that day of birth I had a new awareness that God comes closest when I am in touch with my own weakness.

In the many years since, I have often wanted to hide, but having fallen in love, I can't stay quiet long. The prophet's passion for truth and the poet's vision of what is meant to be keep prodding me to act or open my mouth when it would be safer to remain out of sight, silent.

One time, after a congregational discussion of roles for women and men in church leadership where I spoke what was on my heart, I went home kicking myself. I hadn't spoken with as much finesse as I'd wanted to. *Why do I keep blurting things out? Why do I care so much, then end up wishing I didn't? I will just be quiet,* I decided. *I hate exposing myself to criticism or offending others unnecessarily. It's much easier to hide and I do it well. So hear me, God: I will from now on remain silent.*

Immediately after, I came on Jesus' parable of the talents in Matthew 25:14-30. I saw myself suddenly as the person with the one talent who wanted to play it safe. I saw the master's anger: "You wicked and lazy slave, . . . As for this worthless slave, throw him into the outer darkness." I trembled. Then, and over and over again, when I've wanted to play it safe, the Spirit reminds me it is far safer to risk everything for love than to hide.

More than fifteen years after the encounter with Merton and with a God who comes close to the heart, I agreed with my husband to co-pastor a small church mired in conflict. The church prided itself on being open and progressive. It saw itself as somewhat on the fringe of orthodox Christianity, with an eagerness to explore alternative spiritualities and ways of thinking about God. Many people had left the church in recent years, and those remaining were deeply divided over questions about Jesus, the nature of the church, and pastoral leadership.

Because I had been nurtured by some unorthodox theologies myself and was generally one to agitate for change,

I felt I had the sensitivity and breadth to relate to the group yet keep a vital connection to the center of the church. After years of wrestling with the "tradition of the fathers" and authoritarian mannerisms, I knew I had found some healing and was on the way home. Perhaps I could draw others to where I knew love was lodged.

Things went reasonably well for one year. The church more than doubled in size. Newcomers were drawn to the warmth of the circle where folks were encouraged to be real with each other. And they were drawn to the celebrative, Christ-centered worship. But after the first year I found that my love for Christ and my newborn appreciation for the biblical witness had become a stumbling block for a group of members who resented the focus and direction our leadership had brought to the church. Whereas before I had been one to thumb my nose at orthodoxy and agitate for opening things up, I now found myself in the uncomfortable position of holding the center. How strange to be labeled narrow and authoritarian.

We want this church, my husband and I said, to be a centered community that isn't tossed about and playing chameleon to every latest theological fad. We can only truly "be all things to all people" if we are rooted and grounded in the love of God and the Word of God made known most profoundly in Jesus Christ. To suggest, as some were, that a focus on Jesus Christ was too narrow and that we ought to be more open was to deceive ourselves as to what "openness" means, I said. To be open in this way was to make ourselves available to unnamed and unknown powers.

Liberation can rid us of spirits that oppress us. But if our house is not occupied by the God whom we know in Jesus Christ, squatters of all kinds will take over. As G. B. Caird has written, "The spiritual world, like the natural, abhors a vacuum" (*The Gospel of Luke*, Penguin Books Ltd.,

1963, p. 155). I knew what it was to be "open," I said, and I knew what it was to be passionately in love with the One in whom "all the fullness of God was pleased to dwell" (Col. 1:15-20).

Dissension intensified following this affirmation of what must be central if we were to continue in leadership. Despite much effort to find a common understanding, the congregation's conflict was not happily resolved. In some ways, it would have been easier to be accommodating than to speak the truth as we saw it. For me in particular, it was deeply painful to need to be both pastor and prophet among people we loved. But the conflict forced me to reach for bedrock. Finding it solid, I could stand. And the pain of the ordeal was bearable because of the unsurpassed love of the One to whom I owe my life.

I am still a skeptic. I listen deeply for the integrity of a person or situation, because so many of us act according to a script that doesn't ring true. I don't find it easy to pray or believe that God will intervene to make a difference. For me, faith is a daily discipline, a wager, a bold thrusting of myself into the unknown. But I do it with more and more confidence because love has become, not only that which tenderly reaches in to embrace the me that cowered in fear, but the firm and full center out of which I now offer myself to others. I am at home, and in love, and ready to celebrate.

And I remember how quickly Nathanael's skepticism melted when he came to see Jesus and learned that Jesus already knew him. I imagine him falling to his knees as he said in hushed, awed tones, "Rabbi, you are the Son of God. You are the King of Israel" (John 1:47-49). ■

Sara Wenger Shenk writes of herself, "I was born in Nazareth, Ethiopia. In introducing me, my husband, Gerald, roguishly likes to ask Nathanael's question, 'Can anything good come from Nazareth?' He thinks the answers are obvious. We have between us three mysteriously wonderful children. Much of our married life has been devoted to kingdom living in former Yugoslavia and now in Harrisonburg, Virginia, where I am assistant dean and assistant professor of Christian Education at Eastern Mennonite Seminary. I have authored four books, most recently *Coming Home* (Good Books, 1992) and the forthcoming *Meditations for New Parents*, Herald Press, 1996, co-authored with Gerald). All four deal in some way with the spirituality of the family."

19

Learning to Trust the Lion

Jewel Showalter

I WAS CRYING deep-down sobs into the pillow on the top bunk. I knew any moment I would hear my father call, "It's time to go, children." But I wasn't ready.

It was Sunday afternoon; the hot tropical sun cast a long shadow outside the bedroom window. Somehow I had to get a hold of myself. I decided to stop crying. No more tears. Ever. Enough of this baby stuff. I was nine.

I walked out into the hallway. The dull maroon cement tiles felt cold to my bare feet. I turned a tear-streaked face up to my tall, black-haired father.

"What's wrong, Jewel?" he asked kindly and drew me to his lap in one of our woven twine living room chairs.

"I don't want to go back to boarding school," I said. The tears began again. Big, uncontrollable sobs.

He stroked the flying strands of dark brown hair that had slipped from my two long braids. He waited.

"I know. I don't like that we have to be separated, but I don't know what other options we have for your education here in Ethiopia."

"But, Papa, I'm scared. What if Jesus comes back while I'm at boarding school? What if he takes you and Mama, but I'm left behind?" I felt secure as his long arms encircled my shaking body.

"Jewel, do you want to go along? Do you want to go to heaven?" he asked.

"Of course! Who doesn't?"

He explained that if I asked Jesus to take away my sins, to come into my life as my Savior and Lord, then I would have a Father from whom I would never be separated. We prayed together, and I knew Jesus had received me, that I was his child. My father said Jesus would take me to heaven when he returned. And I believed my father.

This childhood faith was a rock through the many separations my missionary childhood entailed. It was there each time we came home from boarding school for a weekend, then returned for another long stretch. It was there when we came to the United States for our second furlough, when I was fourteen. It was there when my parents returned to Ethiopia for three years and I stayed in the States (along with my two older sisters) for my junior and senior years of high school and my first year of college.

I married a fellow English major, Richard Showalter, and we talked much of what it means to follow Christ—intentional community and missions. Our postgraduate educational pilgrimage took us to the University of Chicago, Goshen Biblical Seminary, and Fuller Theological Seminary. By now we had three young children.

Then Richard came home from a doctor's visit one day and said, "Jewel, he says it's most likely cancer." The diagnosis was confirmed. Testicular cancer. Surgery was scheduled almost immediately.

I sat in the waiting room during surgery fiercely hugging my four-month-old son to my bosom. Surely there was some mistake. How could the God I had given my life to be allowing this illness? It was probably just a test. Like Abraham. It couldn't really be cancer. The doctor came out slowly and removed his surgical mask.

"It was cancer," he said.

"How can you be sure?" I asked.

"I've seen it often enough. I don't know the exact type. We've sent off a specimen. But it looks like a rapidly growing kind. He'll need a second surgery to remove the lymph nodes from his abdominal cavity. Take him home to recover for two weeks, then come in to discuss the second operation. I've recommended you to another specialist."

That was it. But that was enough. My neat, tidy world had fallen apart. The God I had known had let me down.

The next afternoon when the children were all napping, I knelt at the black-and-brown tweed couch in the tiny living room of the Voluntary Service unit house. We were serving as unit leaders during Richard's time of study in the School of World Missions.

I poured out my anger to God. Right now he seemed more like the shifting sands of the Sahara than a rock.

Then I heard his clear unmistakable words to my spirit, "Jewel, you have to trust me."

"Trust you? After what you've done to me? Surely you must be kidding!" I cried in derision. I felt like I'd invested all my money in a certain bank and the bank had gone under. Now the bank manager was calling me and telling me to invest more money.

"Jewel, you have to trust me," the voice persisted.

"How can I?" I agonized. "What is there to trust? I did trust you, but you've proved untrustworthy. Here we are, living sacrificially, preparing for full-time Christian service, and you're pulling the rug out from under us!"

Even though a warm California sun was streaming in through the bird-of-paradise bushes that lined the front of the house, the room seemed dark and cold. I felt abandoned. Did I really believe there was nothing out there? No one who loved and cared, who could be trusted to work for good in all things? Only a big black hole?

The voice came a third time, "Jewel, you have to trust me."

Then I broke before God. "I trust you. I do. I do," I sobbed. "Even if he dies, I'll trust you. You know best. You're in control. I submit to your lordship."

In the days that followed I felt a strength and peace I had never known. As I worked around the unit one morning Luke 9:60 popped into my mind. Not knowing what the text said, I stopped washing dishes and looked it up. "Let the dead bury their own dead," I read, startled, "but as for you, go and proclaim the kingdom of God."

"God, does this mean he's going to die?" I asked, but I sensed nothing. It was then I realized that I'd been so preoccupied with morbid thoughts about his possible death and my position as a young widow with three young children that I'd been paralyzed. I sensed God saying, "Leave thoughts of death. That is in my hands. Follow me!" I did so, with new abandon.

Up to that point I had never been able to pray for Richard's healing. I was trusting God to do what he willed. I dared not believe God would heal Richard—only to be disappointed. So I remained silent on the issue of healing.

The day before he was scheduled to see the second surgeon, we attended a conference where speaker Agnes Sanford encouraged her audience to pray the prayer of faith for the sick. She invited us to move throughout the audience ministering to those around us. Richard began praying for his neighbor.

Then I sensed God's word to my spirit, "Jewel, I want to heal Richard. Ask me."

Trembling and afraid, I moved to his side and cautiously laid my hand on his shoulder. "Jesus, please heal Richard," I whispered.

The next day we met with the doctor. He greeted us kindly and went over the lab report. "The second surgery will not be needed after all," he said. "It's not the kind of cancer we suspected. I'm recommending two weeks of radiation as a precaution, but I'm optimistic about your chances for a full recovery."

Several years later Rosedale Mennonite Missions invited us to pioneer work in Turkey, an experience which again called me to deepen my trust in God. Turkey is a Muslim country which nonetheless is modeled after the secular democracies of Europe. We planned to enter the country as English teachers.

Even though this was a fulfillment of earlier dreams and seemed like the right next step, thoughts of taking our children (ages six, eight, ten) to an unknown country were overwhelming. We began moving ahead. Yet even as we packed final bags and said tearful farewells, my heart was filled with doubts.

"God, please reassure me that we're not making a terrible mistake," I prayed and searched the Scriptures for reassurance. My eyes fell on Psalm 90:1, "Lord, you have been our dwelling place in all generations." That was it. That was what I wanted for my children—a dwelling place in God. Earthly dwellings didn't matter. Let it be an old country farmhouse in Ohio or a high-rise apartment in Istanbul—just let us dwell in God!

I sat on the floor in the cheap Istanbul hotel. I was hunched over a tape recorder, listening to the monotony of a loop tape droning out the unfamiliar Turkish words and sentences I was trying to memorize. The children were restless, eager to get settled in a new home. But we had not yet found an apartment for rent.

The boys began wrestling. I tuned them out, concentrating on the language lesson. But I shouldn't have. Loud sounds of shattering glass ended my study attempts for the day. They had broken the opaque glass door separating our room from the bathroom.

Again I came before the Lord for reassurance. "Are we asking too much of ourselves, our children? Oh, Lord, have mercy. We want to be your message bearers in this foreign country. But are we to be torn apart, shattered in the process?"

Then I saw an unusual picture in my mind's eye. I saw a narrow-necked bottle, the kind people set on a mantel over a fireplace, a bottle filled with the model of a full-rigged sailing ship. But in this bottle there was a big black Bible with gold edging. As the vision faded I meditated on possible meanings. Could it be that God was putting us as his message bearers down the narrow neck of Turkish culture? It felt like we were being torn apart. We couldn't fit. But the God I was learning to trust reassured me that when he does something it is whole, complete, beautiful.

We began to learn the language. Our children attended the local Turkish public schools, even took the required Muslim religious education classes. And God began to bring interested seekers to our door before we felt comfortable praying or leading Bible studies in Turkish.

A small house fellowship began meeting regularly in our home on Sunday afternoons or in the home of a believing Turkish family. Most of the people had never met another Christian, never seen a copy of the Bible. Together we learned to pray, to worship in Turkish. We celebrated our first baptisms in the Mediterranean Sea.

One Saturday Richard left to visit an isolated believer in a city five hours from ours. When night fell he didn't return as he had said he would. The children cried when I tucked them in. They asked, "Where's Daddy?"

"I don't know. But we can trust God." Those were no idle words. I was learning to trust. I slept; when I awoke the words of this hymn were coursing through my mind: "Stayed upon Jehovah, hearts are fully blessed. Finding, as he promised, perfect peace and rest. We may trust him fully all for us to do. They who trust him wholly, find him wholly true" (Frances R. Havergal, 1874).

That day we celebrated worship together without Richard. Guests came and went. Late that night after the children had gone to bed for a second night, not knowing if their father was dead or alive, he returned. He had been detained by the police who were determined to learn why he was in Turkey. They concluded he was a "Christian propagandist" and pressured him for names of other Turkish believers.

As a result of that arrest, Richard lost his job at the university and subsequently our residence permit. We stayed on for another six months working at other jobs, but eventually we were ordered to leave the country within a week.

We quickly disposed of our household possessions, took the children out of school, packed our few trunks, and spent one long last evening with the Turkish believers. We cried and clung to one another, encouraging one another to trust God. One young man spoke God's encouragement into my grief: "Jewel, just remember that someday every knee will bow and every tongue confess that Jesus is Lord."

After our eviction from Turkey, we moved to northern Cyprus and continued visits to the isolated believers in Turkey. God also began to build a church in Cyprus.

Then one day a phone call came from Turkey. A distraught voice on the other end said, "I've heard the police are looking for me. Please pray." Then the line went dead.

Later we pieced the story together. The Turkish police had rounded up believers from Muslim background in all the major cities of Turkey. Although the Turkish constitution guarantees religious freedom, many local police officers take the law into their own hands. Our friends were kept in solitary confinement, blindfolded, and beaten mercilessly. They were called infidels and traitors to their country. They were urged to renounce faith in Christ.

We fasted and prayed for their release. We prayed that

God would keep them strong. Still I secretly wondered if they wished they had never met us. Had we ruined their lives? Finally, after one month of imprisonment, they were released but demoted and ridiculed by the community.

When later I had opportunity to meet a dear Turkish friend (her husband had been imprisoned), I blurted out, "Did you ever wish you had never met us?"

She looked at me amazed. "How can you ask that? We never once thought of turning back. We have gained so much more than we ever lost."

Since then others in their extended families have professed faith in Christ. The gospel continues to spread quietly along kinship and friendship lines.

Why is it so easy to doubt and fear? God is worthy of our trust—and I trust him! Yes, I have known his abiding presence in the traumatic separations of my childhood, in the face of my husband's cancer, in our pioneering among unreached peoples. Indeed I have discovered the truth of what Aslan, the God-lion, told Lucy in C. S. Lewis' children's classic, *Prince Caspian*: "As you grow bigger, I grow bigger." (New York: The Macmillan Company, 1970).

I know "he is not a tame lion." But I intend to cling to his mane—always—sometimes wowed and sometimes weeping. He almost never jumps through the expected hoops, but he always gets there.   ■

Jewel Showalter and her husband, Richard, live in Landisville, Pennsylvania, where they are both active in the ministries of Eastern Mennonite Missions. Richard serves as president, and Jewel works as a writer and church relations resource person. They are involved at University Christian Fellowship, a young, cell-group church which meets on the campus of Millersville University. They are the parents of three young adult children.

20

The Miracle of the Three Plowshares

Shirley Hershey Showalter

> "Where there is great love there are always miracles. . . .
> One might almost say that an apparition is human vision
> corrected by divine love. . . . The Miracles . . . rest not so
> much upon faces or voices or healing power coming sud-
> denly to us from afar off, but upon our perceptions being
> made finer, so that for a moment our eyes can see and our
> ears can hear what is there about us always."
> —Willa Cather, *Death Comes for the Archbishop*
> (Alfred A. Knopf, 1927[1982], p. 50)

IF EVER A MAN were the opposite of a mystic, it was my father, H. Richard Hershey. Daddy liked his rows plowed
straight and his bales stacked neatly in the mow. He was a
man of simple pleasures; the only time I saw something
close to ecstasy on his face was the afternoon the rains
came in a drought. Peeling off the Eby Feeds cap that covered the farmer's tan on his forehead, he began to sing, off-
key but with gusto, "There Shall be Showers of Blessing."
That night he came home and ate nearly two quarts of but-
ter brickle ice cream right out of the box.

The kind of wisdom he dispensed was practical, built
on a solid work ethic. "If it's worth doing, it's worth doing
right." "A good name is better than great riches." "Take the
secretarial courses. Then you can work in a nice bank job

after high school and save up money to buy furniture before you get married."

I was the kind of daughter who didn't always cotton to Daddy's advice, especially his vocational guidance. I had different ideas about the good life and was eager to try them. So every night Daddy and I went through a contest of wills in the cow stable, where he was the boss and I the bullheaded worker. I would enter the limestone barn through the white Dutch doors at 6:00 a.m. and again at 6:00 p.m., reporting for milking duty. Once my mother had to chase me with a broom to get me out of the house. I always took my weapon of choice—a book.

The double row of Holsteins paid scant attention to me as I entered the steamy barn, but Daddy would greet me with my first task, usually feeding all the animals. Then began our tug-of-war. Daddy never let me go along scooping out an average amount of feed to each cow. That would be too easy. He had sound nutritional reasons, he told me, for individualizing his instructions for every step. Cows needed different protein-carbohydrate blends as they went through their yearly cycles of breeding, calving, and weaning.

I would push the feed cart through the path in front of the trough, scoop in one hand, book in the other. Daddy would try to make it impossible to read by giving me a new dinner order every minute or so, but if he waited too long, I'd be engrossed in the world of Jane Eyre or Sidney Carton instead of his. Our feed-trough skirmishes were like a ritual dance, with grudging affection on both sides, but also tension that could erupt occasionally into bursts of temper on his part and resentful huffing and puffing on mine.

The only glimpse I ever got of a father who might understand my desire to enter imaginary worlds instead of cow stables came the night he took me on a date. My mother thought it would be nice for a girl to go on a date with her father before boys with crew cuts and acne started showing up on the doorstep. "Besides," she added, "you won't find a more handsome date anytime soon." She was proud of the way Daddy looked when he changed his coveralls for his one suit, a double-breasted Botany 500 that flattered his muscular six-foot height. With his hair combed smoothly and the fragrance of Old Spice covering any lingering traces of Old Cowstable, he did indeed seem like a worthy escort. I happily climbed into the two-toned green '57 Dodge as he held the door.

We saw the senior play, *Our Town.* Surprisingly, Daddy didn't sleep through it, as he often did through church. As we licked our double ice cream cones at the Twin Kiss afterward, he told me, "Your mother had a vision like that Emily did in the play. After her mother, your grandma Hess, died, she came back and sat in a chair and talked to Mother for a while before she disappeared again."

This piece of news was fascinating to me, not just because I had never suspected either of my parents to have left the plane of the ordinary, but because my father told me this little story with unmistakable respect in his voice. He did not question it any more than he would question the parting of the Red Sea. And though nothing like a mystic event had ever happened to him, he seemed glad, maybe even proud, that he had married someone so blessed by God as to have seen a vision.

Seventeen years after that memorable first date, I returned to the farm with my little son, Anthony, to say good-bye to Daddy for the last time. The fifty-four-year-old man stretched out on a green naugahyde recliner, trying to battle a rare disease that was thickening all his internal organs, did not look like Daddy. Though his hair was still black, his skin was gray and already cold to the touch. Death was only four weeks away, but Daddy had trouble believing it was happening to him. When he awoke from a nap, he would try to sit up, and then he would have to face his weakness all over again. He sat on the edge of the bed, shaking his head, "I can't believe it. I can't believe it. I can't believe it."

Soon after I returned to my Pennsylvania home, Daddy had an attack in the night and had to be rushed to the hospital. Mother and I made daily visits to see him. There he would tell us of highly symbolic dreams, filled with the land and people he knew best but also full of themes of loss and abandonment. Once he was on a tractor in a field and had run out of gas. Mother and my brother and sisters and I were at the end of the row calling to him, but we couldn't help him, and he couldn't get off the tractor.

The life of dreams and the non-dreaming life began to blend in my father's mind and to create a new reality. He was experiencing something he could not communicate fully to us. One morning we arrived to find him in a great state of agitation. He told us that during the night two men dressed in white had come into his room and wanted to take him away. He fought with them and seemed pleased to have won the battle. The hospital staff reported that he had fallen out of bed in the night. Daddy's version of the story led me to imagine the new reality in his mind—a world full of angels of death.

Daddy was a Christian. And I am a Christian daughter with a strong need to believe my father found his way to heaven. Yet I must be truthful. Daddy was frightened by the manifestations of the mysterious that came to him in those intense days in April 1980. And his fear disturbed the rest of us. We needed assurance that faith would dispel fear; we forgot that fear is the beginning of wisdom.

The day after Daddy fell out of bed—or wrestled with angels in the night—he had a great need to talk. Ordinarily, Daddy seldom talked. In fact, he despised "gabbing"—

talk that was not practical, scrupulously truthful, and respectful. He had a rule: "If you don't have anything to say, be quiet." Today he had something to say.

When Mother and I walked into the room, he immediately asked us, "Do you see those three plowshares?"

We looked at each other and shook our heads.

Daddy was not happy with this reply, nor was he satisfied to let the matter rest. "Look," he cried. "There they are. In the middle of the room."

We stepped closer to the place he pointed, peering hard into empty space.

Again, we shook our heads "no."

After a while he gave up, a little disgusted with us. He lost no faith in the fact that the three metal blades were there. He just found us inadequate for the job of seeing them. His eyes had the look of a deer looking into the barrel of a gun. "I don't know why you can't see," he said, riveting his complete attention on us. "But never forget this is real."

Daddy fell back against the pillows propped behind him on the chair. He was sitting next to a window. He began to tell us his latest dream, which involved two pillars of our church, Mel and Janette Wenger. "I was up in a tower, a very high tower, and it was lonely. I didn't want to be there, but I heard beautiful music—anthems—like they sing in the Moravian Church, and that helped. And Mel and Janette were down at the bottom of the tower. They tried to help me, but they couldn't. *It was too much work.*"

I wanted to ask my father what was too much work. But I was afraid of the answer, and he seemed afraid of questions.

Daddy died several weeks later, on May 3, 1980, in the early morning after his fifty-fifth birthday. The next day we held a kitchen-table meeting of the family to plan the funeral. As we selected music, I remembered the word "anthem" that Daddy had used to describe the music in his tower dream. The word had stuck in my mind because it was so unlike the words Daddy usually used. "Anthem" sounded in my ears like a high-church word, and we were distinctly low-church people. But as I paged through *The Mennonite Hymnal,* I came across hymn 312, "Come, Come, Ye Saints," an anthem I had learned from my Goshen College colleague Mary Oyer. I loved it for its vision of a heaven full of singers who "make the chorus swell" singing, "All is well. All is well."

The day of the funeral dawned gloriously for those who could feel it. I was only dimly aware of brilliant yellow light and the smell of blooms in the thick, sweet air. The beauty that surrounded me seemed irrelevant at best and demonic at worst. As the service began, I was thinking about what was unlived in my father's life and what would never be. I was oblivious, therefore, to most of the words floating in the air.

We began to sing "Come, Come Ye Saints." I was seated in the second row on the right immediately behind the casket. The windows of the Lititz Mennonite Church were open to let in the vibrant air. As we sang my favorite phrase in the last verse, "All is well," my head turned toward the open window. Now it was my turn to see a new reality.

Framed precisely in the center of the window to my right were not two, not four, but three plowshares. Adrenalin rushed to every capillary. I whispered to my mother, the only person in the world who could understand, "Look!"

The plowshares were attached to a backhoe. The town was swarming with road-working equipment. In fact, the funeral director had to find a new route to the cemetery because backhoes were digging up Water Street.

As I walked through the cemetery, all of the memories

of visions and of Daddy's blazing eyes came back to me. Now I remembered that in one of his semidream states he had asked my sister Doris if she had had her little girl yet. I was sure the child she was carrying must be a girl (born Abigail Rose Dagen one month later).

I knew that when God gave a sign in the Bible it always changed the destiny of a Mary, a Moses, or a David. I felt all the thrilling terror that accompanies such a visitation from God. But no one answered my question, "What does this mean? What am I supposed to do?" I was like the newly sighted after the blindfolds have come off—overwhelmed by the light and uncertain of my next steps.

The bloody sunset the night of the funeral was as brilliant in crimson as the day had been in gold. I felt pursued by color, afraid to hear and see more. I went indoors to find rest.

The living room, the same room where Daddy's body had lain in state for the viewing and where I had come for my own personal wake in the early morning hours, served as my place of refuge. As I was lying on the sofa, I heard someone in the kitchen talking to my mother.

"I suppose you wonder where Mel and Janette Wenger were today," the visitor said. My ears pricked up immediately upon hearing the names of the only two people Daddy had mentioned in the tower dream. "Janette was going to help us with the meal. We didn't think we could do it ourselves because . . ." I sat up straight, ready to mouth the next words as though I had scripted them—*"it would have been too much work."*

I strained to hear why Mel and Janette weren't at the funeral. "Mel woke up terribly sick this morning, and Janette couldn't leave him home alone." As my mother thanked the visitor for helping in the kitchen and inquired about Mel's fever, I sank back into the sofa cushions, worn out with seeing and hearing the very things I had been unable to see and hear in my father's hospital room, but no more able to understand them when my own senses confirmed their reality than when I had to rely on Daddy's descriptions.

I've carried this story around with me for fourteen years. Until now I had thought there was only one reason I seldom told anyone the story—fear of misunderstanding and ridicule. I had a mystic's secret, and I treasured it, pulling it out to look at it only when I wanted to tell a new friend a story that really mattered or when I wanted to comfort someone who was troubled by his or her own supernatural story. Or who, conversely, sought me out in a time of doubt.

Only when I tried to *write* this story for the first time did I begin to find some new clues to its meaning. I discovered that being with Mother when Daddy told the tower dream and being the only one to see the plowshares in the church had been important parts of this story for me. I thought maybe God would tap me on the shoulder again some day with a hugely important task. Did the world need saving? Perhaps I would lead the charge, following signs and wonders all along the way. In some corner of my brain, I was God's little time bomb, wondering when and how I might explode into a noble calling.

I was and am ashamed to recognize the pride in my secret wish. I had hoped to be special, even though six billion other people on earth have the same wish. I had wanted the miracle to be for Shirley. God wants the miracle to be for everyone.

The plowshares stopped me. They took me out of this world for a second only to bring me back into it more deeply. They directed my attention, which, after fear, is another step on the path toward wisdom. The only ways to hang on to the miracle are to share and to remember. Sharing the miracle means sharing love.

Remembering, for me, means to revisit one perfectly ordinary spring morning—a morning as perfect and as ordinary as all other mornings—and to again feel the wonder as I glance out my window and whisper "Look!"   ∎

Shirley Hershey Showalter is professor of English at Goshen College, Goshen, Indiana, where she lives with her husband, Stuart, also a Goshen professor, and their two children, Anthony, age nineteen, and Kate, age twelve. Her father's last admonition was "Tell the children that Jesus loves them." These words have become a personal mission statement for her work as teacher and mother.

21

Seeking the Face of Jesus

Ronald J. Sider

FROM BIRTH, I was immersed in the best of Anabaptist and Wesleyan piety. It was obvious that Mom and Dad loved Jesus Christ more than anything else. They lived the motto they hung in my bedroom on the second floor of our farmhouse:

> Only one life, 'twill soon be past.
> Only what's done for Christ will last.

Our church—like most other Brethren in Christ congregations in Ontario in the 1940s—had two services on Sunday, a prayer meeting Wednesday evening, and three weeks of revivals every fall and spring. Our family attended almost every service at the Bertie Church. Most if not all of the church people I knew had a simple, honest faith. Adopting that faith as my own came almost naturally.

Our revival tradition insisted, of course, that I must personally make a decision for Christ. At about age eight, during a revival meeting, I walked forward during the altar call, knelt at the front, and asked Jesus to forgive my sins and take charge of my life. I meant it. My life did not change much because I had not been obviously rebellious. But I knew Jesus loved me. I knew I would be with him when he returned. And I wanted to live the way he said we should.

Getting sanctified was harder. The church taught that it

was possible to have the "old sinful nature" completely removed if one asked for the second work of grace. So a number of times during revival meetings, I went forward seeking complete sanctification. I think I was genuinely open to God in that search. But I was also rigorously honest and self-conscious about my inner feelings, thoughts, and desires. And it was painfully obvious to me that my old sinful nature was still very much alive.

I struggled many times through the last verses of "Just As I Am" before I came to understand at about age eighteen or so that sanctification was a process. Finally in graduate school, when I read Martin Luther, I clearly grasped the wonderful truth of justification by faith alone. For the rest of my life, I have enjoyed the solid assurance that I can come into the presence of our Holy God because of Christ's sacrifice on the cross.

I now believe, however, that the core of what my church was trying to say in its emphasis on both discipleship and sanctification was on target. In those years I did decide clearly—both at some especially important times of commitment, and also day by day in the normal struggles of being a teenager—that I wanted Jesus Christ to be the center of my life. I will always be grateful to the Anabaptist and Wesleyan traditions for shaping my life so that I came to truly want nothing, absolutely nothing, to be as important to me as Jesus Christ.

In college, the full force of modern secularism flooded into my comfortable life. I began to doubt whether an honest person in the modern world could really believe in historic Christianity or even the existence of God. I struggled and doubted. Eventually I began to study the Gospels and to ask what a careful historian could say about the early Christian claim that the carpenter from Nazareth was alive on the third day. I discovered that most modern folk—including a lot of biblical scholars—worked with an anti-miracle bias that was really a philosophical prejudice. And I came to see that if one starts in a less biased fashion, the evidence for Jesus' resurrection is as strong or stronger than the evidence for many key events in Greek and Roman history which everybody accepts. By my third year in university, I was again deeply committed to Christ.

I suspect that my deepest, persistent sins have been pride and selfishness. Success has come relatively easy in many areas. My intensely competitive spirit often made up for what I lacked in ability. And I liked to win—whether playing hockey or studying Latin. It appears—although this always amazes me a bit—that some people are spontaneously unselfish. Hardly ever has that been true for me. Whatever unselfish caring and sharing have come into my life have been the result of grace and persistent struggle to be obedient.

My call to be an evangelical "social activist" came in graduate school. There was no loud voice or special experience. But I slowly developed a clear inner sense that I should work as a biblical Christian for peace and justice in society. And opportunities never dreamed about by this Ontario farm boy have come to me in the areas of writing, speaking, and organizing.

I have found it fascinating to see how Satan tries to squeeze into the best things that God allows me to do. After my best speech, when I truly have felt God's presence and power mightily at work, Satan still tries to whisper in my ear, "You really did that one well." I have learned to respond clearly and immediately in my heart, "Dear Father, forgive my arrogance. I want to do everything I do in your power and for your glory. Thank you for working through me."

My toughest battles came where they are supposed to —at midlife and in marriage. I have been blessed with a marriage full of joy, fulfillment, mutual growth, and genuine partnership. Arbutus is a gifted woman who has loved me, affirmed my ministry over the years, and grown herself as a mature partner. Together we chose over the years —in a thousand conscious and unconscious ways—to move from the gentle patriarchy that was common in the church setting of my youth to mutual submission in our marriage. The theory was easier than the practice. Growth was sometimes painful—and slow.

The hardest time came in the late 1970s. We had hurt each other in various ways. Intense anger at Arbutus erupted frequently. Arbutus said we needed marriage counseling, but I was too proud to do that. I told her the other marriages in our fellowship were worse than ours.

The worst time, ironically, was the summer and fall of 1978, when I was preparing the peace lectures for the first national conference of the New Call to Peacemaking. I had scheduled myself too full and had only a few days to write each lecture. Frequently Arbutus and I fell into sharp quarrels, and I regularly became very angry.

More than once I had to start a day of writing my peace lectures with an embarrassed, anguished plea, "Lord, forgive me for my anger at Arbutus. I don't deserve your help in this lecture. But I only have today and I have to write a lot. So please let me understand and write about the biblical call to peacemaking in spite of my fighting with Arbutus."

Before I left for the conference, I promised Arbutus to visit our closest friends on the way home and talk about the problems in our marriage. They convinced me that stubborn, proud Ron Sider needed help. I came home and told Arbutus I was finally willing to go to a Christian counselor. For the rest of our lives, Arbutus and I will be grateful for the wise, solid counsel we received in the next six months.

I also developed a much deeper prayer life in this time

of painful struggle. As I grew up, daily devotions had been part of the expectation for a good Christian. But I had long since concluded that there was no need to be legalistic, though I had also long since discovered that legalism was no longer my problem. In this area, I needed more discipline!

Now my intense sense of need for God's forgiveness, presence, comfort, and power during this time of struggle drove me to my knees more regularly. Far more frequently than in the preceding decade or two, I started the day with prayer. I begged for forgiveness. I cried out in pain. I pleaded with God for help. These times in the presence of God became a comfort and strength in a way I had never before experienced. Probably for the first time in my life, I came really to enjoy my devotional time.

That deeper joy and desire for personal time alone in God's presence continues to be part of my life. Seldom do I go with the same sense of pain and need. Thank God that renewed wholeness and peace have returned to my relationship with Arbutus. I still have to *choose* to discipline myself and decide to make time for devotions in my busy schedule. But in that tough time of struggle, I developed a pattern and discovered a joy that makes it somewhat easier to be disciplined more often than in the past.

As I approach fifty-six, my deepest longing and desire is to obey and glorify my Lord Jesus whom I love and worship. In my youth, I used to fear that total, unconditional surrender to Christ would mean sacrifice and loss. Today I have a certainty at the center of my being that unqualified submission to the risen Lord Jesus is the way to the deepest joy and fulfillment.

I still struggle with temptation. But when it comes, I turn it over to Christ and seek his presence and power. My prayer is that as the years unfold I can look more and more, as Paul says in 2 Corinthians 3:18, directly into the face of my Lord. I want to reflect his glory into a broken world. I long to be changed—yes, sanctified—so that day by day I may be transformed more and more into his likeness.   ■

Ronald J. Sider is professor of theology and culture at Eastern Baptist Theological Seminary in Philadelphia and president of Evangelicals for Social Action. Though his personal vocation has been to call evangelical Christians to greater awareness of the social dimensions of the gospel, he seeks to promote and live a wholistic gospel, including both social concern and evangelism. This passion is reflected in his recent book, *One-Sided Christianity*. His best known book is *Rich Christians in an Age of Hunger* (Word Inc., 1991). His speaking and writing have found a large audience internationally among a wide range of Christians.

22

Letting Go in Belleville

Arnold Snyder

> "In the beginning was the Word, and the Word was with God, and the Word was God. [The Word] was in the beginning with God. All things came into being through [the Word], and without [the Word] not one thing came into being. What has come into being in [the Word] was life, and the life was the light of all people."—John 1:1-4

THESE WORDS from John the Evangelist are gospel to me; they are the good news. My experience has been that there is a powerful, life-giving, and creative current running through this universe that we inhabit. I don't have words adequate to express this reality, although I can and do use religious language to point to it. I speak of Spirit, the Word, or God.

Although I have known this Christian language all my life, I never really experienced the reality to which those words point until I was an adult. I think the word "creativity" gets at some of what has happened to me when I have come into contact with this power of life. I have experienced this living current of life speaking to me in a number of different worlds and in the various languages spoken in those different worlds.

I grew up as a missionary kid. I was first converted at age five. I was baptized at age six, by a Mennonite missionary, into a church that says it doesn't believe in infant baptism. I have been converted several times since, so I have been able to put my first conversion into perspective.

As a five-year-old, I was frightened by the world I heard described—in vivid language—at that Sunday night revival meeting in tropical Puerto Rico. The preacher painted a picture of a world of judgment, of hell, of fiery pits and eternal suffering. I was already hot and sweaty; I was also terrified. Within the limits of my tender years, I understood well that I was a sinner and that I deserved this eternal punishment. I knew that I had done wrong things; and I definitely didn't want to spend eternity in a fiery pit.

So I raised my hand at the altar call to set everything right and avoid the dire consequences. I was told I had been saved. I was relieved and thoroughly happy for a good while; I remember reading my Spanish Bible perched up in the branches of my favorite guava tree and feeling good about it all.

I think I understood that religious world as well as any five-or-six-year-old can. I understood the language, and I learned to speak that language. It gave me entrance into a particular world and interpretation of Christian belief. I think that my conversion was genuine, within those limits.

I am the father of five children, the youngest now six. This means I have had five chances to observe children passing through the ages of five and six, and I have had to ponder—more than once—what conversion to Jesus Christ might mean to them.

I have not introduced my children to the language of this frightening world of damnation and salvation. Maybe the reason is that my commitment to that language and worldview lasted only as long as the fear of damnation and the hope of salvation from hell were convincing. When I was no longer afraid, I left it all behind—the good with the bad.

Around the time of puberty I discovered my body in an immediate and urgent way. I set out to learn the language of the body with the zeal of a new convert. Here was a whole new world *really* worth learning. The old spiritual world of hell and damnation faded into the background. It had no more power over me. I didn't give a rip. I simply didn't believe in that world any more. It wasn't real; what my body was telling me *was* real. And a lot more interesting. I was amazed at the sensual possibilities offered by my body and the language it spoke.

I don't think I was unusual. Nor do I think sensual discovery is an evil, nasty thing. To the contrary, we don't inhabit a world of pure souls or pure ideas. We are only whole and complete beings when we recognize and embrace our full humanity, including our physical and sensual dimensions. I only understood much later that the Christian story also has words for this physical, sensual side of our experience: God took on human flesh. There is an "incarnation" at the heart of the Christian story of salvation.

As a young person, however, I found that the world of the body and the languages of the senses were sufficient. I wanted and needed no theology to interpret that world. It stood on its own. What mattered was the *now*. What mattered was living, being, feeling, loving, experiencing, in all the richness I could manage. In the middle of such euphoria, salvation from sin—which I had come to understand as salvation from physical misdeeds—was meaningless. I simply didn't *want* to be saved from my body at all. And if the time came to die, I hoped to have packed in plenty of living in the meantime, since I was convinced it was the only reality worth having anyway.

With the benefit of the distance time provides, I can think of these worlds and languages as two poles at opposite extremes of my life experience. It now seems to me that the attitudes embodied in both of those extreme experiences were more negative than positive. The first attitude was one that was certain its language of faith had the answers to all the mysteries of life. But it achieved that certainty by placing strict limits on life, language, and experience. Looking back, living in that little world was like trying to live in a stifling, airless room with food periodically shoved under the door in controlled doses.

But equally tragic to me now is the frame of mind that did not know or recognize any reality or language beyond physical experience. I lived in that world as well. That second, youthful, I-centered world with its sensual language appeared liberating—especially in contrast to the first world of locked doors and drawn curtains—but in reality it was not. To change the image, living in that second world was like rowing hard with one oar. There was plenty of frenzy in pursuit of narrow goals. Rowing with one oar means a lot of activity and splash, but you circle around yourself.

Learning another language, that of improvisational music, helped open the way for my introduction to the *living* God. As a young person, I devoted myself full-time to learning blues and jazz. What I discovered was that at certain crucial moments—and they could not be programmed—the music began to play itself. Those of us playing our instruments became almost spectators. There was a creative current present in those moments that all of us recognized. It involved a certain letting go that had to happen for all of us. The experience was so amazing, so energizing, so incredible that I devoted a good part of my life to pursuing it.

Somewhere in all the craziness of that life, there was someone accompanying me, although I didn't recognize this till later. And the lessons I was learning at the keyboard—about letting go and trusting the creative power—were preparing me for a larger and more significant letting go.

One night outside Belleville, Ontario, I was lying in my bed after the usual show, about to go to sleep, when I became aware of a powerful presence around and in me. I was frightened. I was aware of a living being, a powerful current that possessed more life and power than I had ever known. At the same time, I was enfolded by love.

I don't have words that come close to explaining what happened, although I have tried. No words were spoken, but the power or presence clearly asked me this: Was I ready to let go of myself, to surrender myself, to follow? The love and power invited me, but it also asked something in return which I was loath to relinquish: my self.

I felt I could have said no to that love and power, and a part of me very much wanted to. I was afraid of what I was losing. I hesitated. I experienced dread. I was afraid to say yes and afraid to say no. But there was no time to analyze or ask rational questions. Finally I said *yes*—not in words but in my inmost self. I yielded; I let go in trust.

What was this "something" that found me, at the age of twenty-five, in a hotel in Belleville, Ontario, after a night of rock and roll music and exotic dancers? Who was this "someone" to whom I gave my life in the very core of my being? I can *point* to this something or someone with language. I can and do call it God, the Lord of the universe, the Creator, the one whom Jesus called "Abba."

But I have a strong urge to resist these handy designations. If I say that "God" found me and converted me, I am telling the truth. But I fear that those who hear this language will immediately translate it into the familiar, habitual, ritual speech of churches and church institutions. And I am sorry, but this will not do. The "cookie cutter" language of faith doesn't begin to touch the power, the mystery, the living reality that consumed and changed my life.

Because my firsthand experience of divinity took place in a sleazy bar, and not in a Christian revival meeting, I had no context, language, or ready vocabulary for that event. After I had been found by divinity, I discovered that all kinds of religious and nonreligious languages, in many different contexts and worlds, seemed to point to aspects of the reality I had experienced. I understood what had been incomprehensible to me as a young person—why people might want to spend time doing something called "worship." I understood why people could speak the language of conversion. My own life turned around that night, and I began a new walk, a new conversation, a new exploration in undreamed of directions that finally have led me here.

One aspect of that new walk and exploration now seems amazing to me, although it felt natural at the time: it was a *guided* exploration. My steps were being directed, day by day, one at a time, toward an end. But I had no *name* for what I was experiencing. I would say now that I spent much time in intense prayer—but at the time I didn't use such language. I simply "spoke" inwardly to the reality before whom I had bowed and offered my life, and I asked to be guided.

Perhaps I had learned to do this as a child, thanks to my upbringing, but I was not aware that I was "praying," since what I was doing then bore so little relationship to the prayer I had known. This conversation was a dialogue with a living being who knew me intimately. Prayer as I had known it had been mostly words mumbled in the general direction of heaven.

But the living conversation guided me, step by step, in miraculous ways. It led me out of one way of life into another, out of destructive relationships into other positive and fruitful ones. Eventually I found Jesus, too, although only along the road of a long process and search. I look back over those years now and, using theological language, can see that the providential hand of God was working in my life. But at the time I didn't have the language for it: it was just a living, spiritual adventure.

What was it like, that divinity I experienced? It was like a pearl of great price—once you know that it exists, you sell all you have to get it. It was maybe like a mustard seed —a little thing that grows and grows, and before you know it, it has taken over your life.

I used to believe that virtually all faiths led to the divinity, and that it did not much matter which path of faith a person chose, since the end was the same. My mind was not changed because of the exclusivist claims made in the Bible about the only way to the Father. Nothing as rationally and literally self-confident as that has affected me.

I started to change my mind because I started to lose my way in the maze; I could no longer follow. I realized that, even if the universalist statement were true, I still could not walk all paths at the same time, running from one to the other on the basis of the latest book I had read. A spiritual exploration and walk that was directed "to whom it may concern" was not getting me very far. I had to choose *a* path (or did the path choose me?) and begin the exploration in earnest.

It was in this rather backhanded manner that I returned to Christianity and to the church—first to the Anglican communion, then through Anabaptist studies, back to the Mennonite church. I came back to my family of faith, to my people, to my home. I came back to Jesus.

But either Jesus had changed, or I had changed. He was no longer simply the historically correct, blessed Savior who rescued humanity from eternal damnation by atoning for sin. Jesus was no longer simply an affirmation of faith. I could, did, and do affirm this language, in full conscience; but remaining with just these historical affirmations was like living on thin gruel. More fundamentally for me, I came to know Jesus as the living power that had convicted me of sin in my deepest being and had shown me what true forgiveness and liberation from sin meant.

To announce this *living* Jesus is to preach the gospel. Jesus is the power of the Creator incarnate—present in the man Jesus, and present today. Jesus the Christ, truly God and truly human. And God is in Jesus the Christ, reconciling humanity to the Creator.

I have found no recipe for retaining, let alone teaching, the language of living faith. I myself keep forgetting and having to relearn it over and over. But this much I know: At the heart of that language and that world is learning to trust, learning to let go of our need for control, overcoming fear, and being ready to live with the consequences of truthfulness. At the heart of this language of living faith is a love without measure that surrounds us, flows into us, and overflows out from us.

There is an unmovable measure, a plumb line, which does not fail. It is the love and presence of Jesus. Does our language shed light on or obscure that unfathomable love? Does the language that guides our lives lead us deeper into the love of Jesus, which constantly reaches out to us and to all of God's children? Truly blessed are those who learn to be measured by the living love of Jesus.

The living Word that was from the beginning speaks all languages and inhabits all worlds. We do not own it or control it.

We cannot imagine how to market it. The boxed and bottled savior offered in the marketplace is not likely to be the living God—although based on my experience, I would not entirely rule out that possibility!

But in the end, I believe that there is no technique for learning the language of living faith because it is a gift. We can learn to be open and receptive to receiving a gift. But the gift itself remains a gift and a surprise; it is not a payment handed out to those technically proficient in religious languages.

Still we have every reason to continue our walk in a spirit of hope and expectation. The Creator is not stingy; the living Word speaks daily and hourly, in manifold ways, for those whose eyes and ears are prepared to see and to hear. My prayer is simply this: May we continue to look and listen. May we open ourselves, with as much fearlessness as we can manage, to life, to truth, to creativity, to love, and to beauty—in whatever worlds we are ready and able to find them, in whatever languages we are able to speak and which speak to us. I am certain that the loving power of life, truth, and beauty will also find us—mind, body, and soul.   ■

Arnold Snyder is married to Linda Lou King; they are the parents of two daughters and three sons. Arnold has taught history at Bluffton College (1979-1984) and directed Witness for Peace in Managua, Nicaragua (1984-1985). He currently teaches church history and peace and conflict studies at Conrad Grebel College, Waterloo, Ontario.

23

From Road to River Spirituality

Erland Waltner

AS I WRITE this, I am seventy-nine, basically retired from fifty-five years of ministry with the General Conference Mennonite Church, gradually losing my eyesight due to macular degeneration, yet still actively involved in a part-time role at the Associated Mennonite Biblical Seminary in Elkhart, Indiana.

Sixty-five years ago I first confessed my faith in Jesus Christ, was baptized into the Salem Mennonite Church at Freeman, South Dakota, claimed forgiveness for sins. I began reading the Bible avidly as a teenager and began to struggle with a sense of call from God to enter some kind of "full-time Christian service," as we called it then. I pursued what I now call a spirituality of direction or guidance. I sincerely wanted to know God's will for my life. Until then, I had been inclined to seek God primarily when I was in some kind of trouble, as when my younger brother was near death with pneumonia.

Since then I have traveled many roads serving as pastor, college Bible teacher, visiting biblical preacher, and later as seminary teacher and administrator. My activities log includes literally thousands of sermons and even more classroom hours, not to mention board and committee meetings at virtually every level of organized church life. During all these years and in all of these ministries, I have spoken often and much, with earnestness and even with passion, of God, of Jesus Christ, and of the Holy Spirit.

During the last decade of my life, however, I have sensed that I am again in transition in my experience of God. This has come about in part because I have been in a conscious occupational retirement process. It has also come because I have experienced in a new way how important spiritual life disciplines are for me.

Such disciplines include for me especially regular times and patterns of prayer, deliberate and structured meditative reading of Scripture, keeping a spiritual life journal, and sharing monthly with a person who has consented to be a spiritual guide to me.

In this transition I am aware that for many years of my Christian life and ministry, my time with God was something like a quick stop while driving hard on a long and sometimes rough road. I have compared it to a pit stop in the Indianapolis 500 when racers stop to refuel, to check tires, to watch for possible trouble ahead before hurrying back into the fast lane as quickly as possible. God has truly been gracious in keeping me from crashing, but I now also know that I missed out on much God was eager to give me even during those busy years of congregational, conference, and institutional work. I was a hard driver, sometimes driving family and colleagues into undue stress. I called mine "a spirituality of the road."

Now I am beginning to see my relationship with God as being more like a river which helps me get from here to there, and also actually helps *carry me* along from day to day, from task to task, from one experience to the next. I am experiencing God as One who is not only daily present with me but One who is in motion, bearing me up, sustaining, renewing, enabling me.

Prayer times are now, not only pit stops to refuel, but also times of overwhelming gratitude, of buoyant reassur-

ance, and of growing hope as well as times of asking, seeking, and knocking for myself or for others in intercession.

In retrospect, I wish I had experienced these aspects of
prayer long ago. However, I now also confess that this
kind of awareness of God calls for something I may not
have been ready for earlier. It involves what Richard Rohr
has called a "spirituality of subtraction," that is, a spirituality of letting go and letting God.

Much of our lives is devoted to accumulation of cogni-
tive knowledge, of social relationships, of material hold-
ings—but the call of God is also to the simplification of life,
to letting go, to yielding up, to a detachment from what
sometimes become our addictions. This the rich young
ruler refused to do and thus remained very sad.

Spirituality of the river, as I now like to call it, asks for a
higher kind of trusting in God than I earlier experienced
when I was more inclined to cover all the bases to protect
my interests. I used to have a kind of inward satisfaction
about trying to keep my life under control, especially my
own control. I tended to rationalize that I must be a pru-
dent provider for my family and a responsible steward of
all that God and God's people had entrusted to me. I tended to push my sense of responsibility beyond appropriate
boundaries.

Spirituality of the river also calls for a deeper kind of
love in which I am more ready to give up more willingly
and gracefully than before things that once were important to me. This includes proper recognition of things I ac-
complished (by God's grace, to be sure). I was vaguely an-
noyed by an observation I heard long ago, that "you can
do a lot of good in the world if you don't mind who gets
the credit for it." Now I'm beginning to grasp more deeply
what it means truly to love God with my whole being, and
my neighbors, including my enemies, as myself.

This spirituality also calls for a profound hope that,

even while I can no longer have what I once had, what ultimately matters in life is entirely secure in and with God. To abound in hope, when so many around me wallow in despair, strikes me as a divine calling precisely for such an ominous time as this.

Learning to be carried on and by this river is no easier than learning to swim in the first place, a skill I have never really mastered. I perceive myself as being still in an early stage of learning to let go and let God.

This formula—letting go and letting God—has two parts, not only one. Both parts require deep faith and love and hope. It is hard and even painful to let some things go. But so is it to let God be God, truly God, in my life. That seems to confront so directly the currently popular moods of self-assertiveness and self-actualization. It surely challenges the current cult of narcissism.

To be honest, then, I must say that I have only started on this part of my spiritual journey, but I am clear in my heart that this is the way I must go. To me it is exciting and reassuring that many others have found this way—the spirituality of the river—long before I came along and will find it long after I am gone.

Meanwhile I identify with the way Susan W. N. Ruach describes this "New Way of Struggling."

> To struggle used to be
> To grab with both hands
>   and shake
>   and twist
>   and turn
>   and push
>   and shove and not give in
> But wrest an answer from it all
> As Jacob did a blessing.
> But there is another way
> To struggle with an issue, a question—

Simply to jump off
> into the abyss
> and find ourselves
>> floating
>> falling
>> tumbling
>> being led
> slowly and gently
> but surely
> to the answers God has for us—
> to watch the answers unfold
> before our eyes and still
> to be part of the unfolding.

But, oh! the trust necessary for this new way!
Not to be always reaching out
For the old hand-holds.

(In Reuben P. Job and Norman Shawchuck, *A Guide to Prayer*, Nashville: Upper Room, 1983, pp. 331-332. Used by permission of the author.)

Cautious by nature and endowed with a large dose of critical reasoning, I find it hard to jump. However, I am learning that when it is truly God who says, "Jump," it is human folly not to let go. To hold on to privilege, advantage, and earnings seems so safe, so just, and so reasonable. But to let go yields peace and joy and wholeness beyond expectation.

Meanwhile, in the midst of a shame-troubled culture, I affirm with all my heart with the apostle Paul, "For I am not ashamed of the gospel; it is the power of God for salvation to everyone who has faith" (Rom. 1:16).

And again,

> For this gospel I was appointed a herald and an apostle and a teacher, and for this reason I suffer as I do. But I am not ashamed, for I know the one in whom I have put my trust,

and I am sure that he is able to guard until that day what I have entrusted to him. (2 Tim. 1:11-12)

This is the good news I am experiencing in new depth. Thanks be to God. ∎

Erland Waltner, president emeritus of Mennonite Biblical Seminary, Elkhart, Indiana, has also been a pastor; a church and conference leader, including Mennonite World Conference; and a college and graduate-level Bible teacher. In active retirement he served as part-time executive for the Mennonite Medical Association, while continuing also part-time as a seminary teacher. Currently he is working on a commentary on 1 Peter for the Believers Church Bible Commentary series.

24

Lost and Found

Katie Funk Wiebe

PEOPLE get lost in various ways. Once, when I was about ten or eleven, I became separated from my friends in a strange city. Almost my whole village in northern Saskatchewan had driven the sixty miles to the city to celebrate the long-awaited visit of King George VI and Queen Elizabeth of England. In the tremendous crush of people, as we youngsters rushed to and fro to catch yet another glimpse of these special guests, I got lost. Alone, I had to find my way back to a relative's home where my parents were waiting.

I had one landmark: a large flour mill that loomed tall on the horizon miles from where I stood. I knew it was close to where I was going. I headed in that general direction.

On either side of the street, as I walked, house after house taunted me in my lostness. My legs grew wearier, my spirit more downcast with each step. I wanted to crawl into the cracks in the sidewalk with the ants. They at least knew where they were going. The flour mill never got closer.

I was overcome by the bleak feeling that no amount of cheerfulness or courage could help me find the way back. I was lost. Finally a kindly policeman noticed my plight and redirected me. I could go home again.

Another time, while swimming with some cousins in an indoor saltwater swimming pool, I managed to make my way to a center island with the support of friends. But they returned to the shallow end without me. I couldn't swim, and wading was out of the question—the water was over my head. I knew I was drowning, but I hadn't done enough swimming to know that all I had to do was holler for help.

As I floundered, the salty water cut the back of my throat and nose and pained my eyes. I reached and reached for the handrails. My toes stretched to touch bottom but found no footing. The pool was bottomless. Gasping, weary, and humiliated, I made it to safety. I never told anyone about the experience.

But my lostness hasn't always been geographical or physical. It has also been spiritual. Each time I experience anew the same awful feeling I had as I walked endlessly, not finding my relative's home; as I sank endlessly, not finding the bottom. Then finally comes the sight of a familiar house and the wonderful touch of handrails.

I grew up in a little immigrant village whose citizens came from many nationalities and creeds, including Russian, Doukhobor, English, Scottish, Irish, French, Ukrainian, Indian, Polish, and German. They were all there as well as some I have forgotten.

Our community was not particularly religious, but a few churches stood at the corners of the town, keeping evil at a distance. There was a Roman Catholic church with a 7:30 a.m. bell calling its many members to mass; a United Church of Canada with a good-sized Sunday school, a dwindling Ladies Aid, and a small attendance at other services; an Anglican church in which a visiting minister held services once a month; a Russian Baptist church in the country with joyous singing; and a Doukhobor Hall attended by the colorfully shawled and many skirted babushkas and their families.

"Being a believer" (*glänbig*) was important to my German immigrant parents. You either believed in Jesus Christ as Savior or you didn't. But churchgoing was needed for respectable living, and since our own denomination wasn't represented in the community, we lived a double life. In summer we were Mennonite Brethren and attended church across the river. In winter, when the river froze and roads were snowed over, Mother and Dad were Russian Baptist and we children, who couldn't understand Russian, were United Church. It seemed a fairly satisfactory arrangement for all.

But this circumstance—living with the "heathen" on the wrong side of the river—meant we Funk children and other Christians in the community were evangelized along with all the openly sinful people by those on the "Christian" side of the river.

The Salvation Army, with large band or small ensemble, frequently held street meetings in our community on Saturday evenings. Even if Mother had already twisted my hair in rags to make curls for Sunday services, I rushed the half-block to the bank corner when I heard the tambourines and trumpets. I pushed my way through the crowd to where I could see and join in the singing.

The Western Children's Mission, with headquarters about twenty-five miles away across the river, regularly sent teams of young people to teach vacation Bible school (VBS) in rural schools in our area. I attended gladly. I memorized Bible verses and usually won at Bible sword drill. This was fun. I learned it was important to have Jesus in my heart. This event had to happen at a specific time, a specific place, and with a specific Scripture verse to base one's faith on. I also learned there was a special language that went along with being a Christian that had to be learned. Ordinary language wouldn't do.

One day after a VBS class, burdened by my need to become a Christian, I rushed upstairs to the family's one small closet. I buried my head in Mother's nightgown, which usually hung there. I prayed urgently, "Come into my heart, Lord Jesus; come into my heart, Lord Jesus."

Nothing. Absolutely nothing. I didn't know the magic words. The comforting smell of Mother clung to the gown. I went out to play.

One New Year's Eve, after hearing much about the coming of the end of the world on that night, I crawled into bed reluctantly. The world would end and I was not saved. I really didn't know what to do. I dug deeper into the sleep-welcoming comforter next to my sister and waited, terrified. Sleep won. The next morning the sun bounced generous rays off sparkling crystals of snow and assured me all was right with the world.

I wanted to make things right with God, but I didn't know the right words. Was I a Christian or wasn't I? Was I lost or saved? Which side did I belong to?

The summer I was twelve, our family attended revival meetings at the Russian Baptist church. These meetings usually caused serious heart pounding when the altar call was given. You were expected to go to the front at least once when you were young. I don't know what the preacher said except that he thundered his message mightily with much pulpit thumping.

I went to the front, where the preacher pronounced me a child of God. Now I was really saved. At home my parents kissed me and wished me well. I was on the right road. But next day I was back to square one. I expected at least a few neon lights, a few loud bells. What happened next? No instructions came with this package of salvation.

By a strange set of circumstances, when I began working in the city after high school, I found myself living in the family quarters of the owner of a convalescent home as her paying guest. Her daughter and I shared a room.

Perhaps living so close to older frail adults who had

lost their firm grip on life caused me to think seriously that summer. Life was busy with dating, going to movies, playing tennis—but it was dull. I had a job, but all it did was provide money for living expenses. I called myself a Christian, but I wasn't a disciple. Even reading had become boring, though I carried home armloads of books from the library, hoping to find something to fill the void in my heart. But the words I read were all empty, falling like chaff before the wind.

Weeks went by. I could not understand the discomfort I was experiencing. I believe now it was the working of the Spirit. The aching God-hole inside needed to be filled.

One Saturday morning I was bookless. Like a caged animal, I wandered about, searching for something to do. Finally in the sunroom, as I rummaged through untidy shelves of old books and papers, I came on a grubby-looking book with cheap pulp-paper pages. As I carelessly leafed through it, I noticed it was a religious book. Any book was better than no book, so I took it to my room.

The book turned out to be a volume of daily devotional readings, something I had never come across before. So in much the same way as I had often sought a penny fortune in a slot machine, I turned to September 1 to read what had been written for that day. The words of Scripture leaped from the page. " 'Ye shall be holy; for I am holy' (1 Peter 1:16 [Revised Version, 1881]). Continually restate to yourself what the purpose of your life is. The destined end of [humankind] is not happiness nor health, but holiness."

To find the right words for the right moment is as exciting as finding a hidden gold mine. I stared at the words as ideas tore loose and raced in all directions within me. This book I clutched in my hand was telling me what I wanted to know. I read quickly, eagerly, to the end of the page. "God has one destined end for [humanity] viz., holiness.

His one aim is the production of saints. God is not an eternal blessing-machine . . . ; he did not come to save [us] out of pity: he came to save us because he had created [us] to be holy."

That day my weak, faltering faith received strength. My aimless feet were put on course. My ambitionless life was given a goal. A lost sheep was found. A rebellious spirit yielded to a Master. Godliness, not getting blessings from God, was God's goal for my life. I can't explain even now what happened then, but I experienced a renewal of spirit.

I now knew where I belonged—with the Christian community serving God. I was no longer lost. I recall the hunger I had those early days to know more about God's Word. The next fall I quit my job and left for Bible college.

Much as I would have liked to keep the book for myself, I returned it to the shelf in the sunroom after typing a copy of the reading for myself. (I still have it.) I forgot, however, to write down the title of the book. Several years later a friend presented *My Utmost for His Highest* by Oswald Chambers to my husband and me as a wedding gift. When within a few weeks, I came upon the familiar selection for September 1; I recognized the book I thought was lost to me forever. Since then I've dipped into all kinds of devotional books but soon drop them to return to the timeless writings of Chambers.

Soon after I found the book, I became an active member of the local youth group. We were the "Jesus" people of our time, during World War II, when "youth fellowships" of every nature and description blossomed across the country. The will of God for our lives, Christ's love for humanity, fellowship, Bible study, and missions became our passion.

I recall those years fondly. We were simplistic perhaps, somewhat overeager, but I believe the church needs such uncritical joy and vigor to carry on before the "let's examine this more carefully" period develops.

For years I found it difficult to speak about my "conversion" openly. It didn't match what was expected in the evangelical world of my time which asked for an intense experience of conviction of sin, a sudden turning based on a verse of Scripture, and a fast switch in character. My movement toward God had been slow, over an entire winter and summer. Reading the book had been the incentive to clinch the direction I was going.

But my life was changing in the direction of godliness. That was obvious. My goals, my thoughts, my actions had changed. I assured myself, silently at first, and gradually louder and louder: "I am a Christian. God's Spirit works in many ways, over many spans of time. It is only we humans who try to confine God to a small box we can control." I wanted a relationship with a big God. A powerful God. A renewing God. Keeping God out of that little box has become a lifelong task.

But I never turned back. I had found the house, the handrails. Still better, I had been found.   ■

Katie Funk Wiebe of Wichita, Kansas, loves storytelling, explaining difficult biblical truths in simpler language, and encouraging people to write about the riches in their past. She taught English at Tabor College, Hillsboro, Kansas, for twenty-four years and is now a freelance writer and editor. She has written or edited fourteen books and had hundreds of articles published. Her most recent books are *Border Crossing* (Herald Press, 1995) and *Prayers of an Omega* (Herald Press, 1994). She has also written/edited *Life After Fifty: A Positive Look at Aging in the Faith Community* (Faith & Life Press) and written *Bless Me Too, My Father* (Herald Press). She attends the First Mennonite Brethren Church in Wichita, where she is active in adult ministries. She has four children and five grandchildren.

Appendix: Who Are the Mennonites?

MENNONITES in 1990 were scattered across the globe and numbered about 850,000 members. About 380,000 lived in North America (*Mennonite World Handbook, 1990: Mennonites in Global Witness,* p. 327).

Mennonite groups have their origin in the Protestant Reformation of the sixteenth century. Though they were originally called "Anabaptists" (re-baptizers) by their opponents, the main stream of the movement soon became known as "Mennonites," after an important early Dutch leader of the Anabaptists, Menno Simons.

The Anabaptists practiced adult baptism because they believed that only those who had chosen voluntarily, personally, to be followers of Christ should be church members and that baptism should be the sign of that decision. Such adult baptism was, from the perspective of the Anabaptists, the only real baptism. But from the perspective of the Roman Catholic Church, into which virtually everyone had already been baptized as an infant, adult baptism was "re-baptism."

The focus on the church as body of adult believers committed to the way of discipleship, which lay behind the baptismal practice of the Anabaptists, was a distinctive feature of the group. They saw the church as a body which gathers, not only to worship, but also to come to understand together what Christ's will is for daily life—"discernment."

They agreed with Martin Luther that we are made right with God only through God's grace forgiving our sins, but they believed that truly experiencing this grace would also result in following after the way of Jesus in life. This discipleship for them typically included mutual assistance to one another in matters of economics, rejection of any participation in warfare or violence, and separation from "worldly" things such as drunkeness and sexual immorality. The church was to be a body of those who walked this path of discipleship.

The Anabaptists' conception of the church, their rapid growth in the early years of the movement, their condemnations of what they saw as errors and abuses in established churches, and their understanding of discipleship (particularly their rejection of "the sword," or warfare, for Christians) made them threatening to other major Christian groups, Catholic and Protestant alike. In many areas, they were severely persecuted and thousands were martyred.

Before many decades, they had become fairly withdrawn small groups scattered across Europe, and for several centuries significant numbers of them migrated to different lands where they were promised both greater freedom to practice their religious beliefs and access to land. Mennonites first came to North America in the late seventeenth century, and many others have arrived in various waves since.

As a result of diverse histories (geographically, linguistically, etc.), disagreements on specific meanings of discipleship, and theological and personality conflicts, Mennonites in North America are divided into a number of different "conferences" or semi-denominational groupings.

The spread of Mennonites outside Europe and North

America, and outside of "traditional Mennonite" families, began in earnest in the late nineteenth century as Mennonites became more accepted in their societies and less withdrawn. An enormous range of institutions have been spawned among North American Mennonites, including schools at all levels, hospitals, mental health facilities, insurance companies, service organizations, and mission boards.

A variety of foreign mission programs resulted in Mennonite-related churches on every continent. At present there are about equal numbers of Mennonites (though they sometimes go by different names) in Europe and North America combined and in the rest of the world. Mennonite churches are growing rapidly in parts of Africa, Asia, and Latin America. Mennonite World Conference provides a context for fellowship and relationship among widely diverse Mennonites globally.

Increased cooperation among Mennonites marks our twentieth-century history. The two largest North American Mennonite groups, the Mennonite Church and the General Conference Mennonite Church, work closely together on many projects and are committed to integration.

The chief cooperative undertaking of North American Mennonites, however, including a much wider range of groups, is Mennonite Central Committee (MCC). It is a relief, service, and development agency with programs in more than fifty countries and with close to one thousand full-time workers, many volunteers, and hundreds of persons hired to work in its programs in their own countries. MCC's purpose is to be "a Christian resource for meeting human need." All MCC work is done "in the name of Christ."

For more information about Mennonites see:

1. C. J. Dyck, *An Introduction to Mennonite History* (Scottdale, Pa.: Herald Press, 1993), for a general history.

2. *Mennonite World Handbook, 1990: Mennonites in Global Witness*, Diether Götz Lichdi, ed. (Carol Stream, Ill.: Mennonite World Conference, 1990), for glimpses of recent Mennonite experience and thought globally and for statistics about Mennonite groups.

3. J. Howard Kauffman and Leo Driedger, *The Mennonite Mosaic*, (Scottdale, Pa.: Herald Press, 1991), for a sociological study of Mennonites in North America.

4. *The Mennonite Encyclopedia* (Scottdale, Pa.: Herald Press, 1955-1959, 1990), for articles on the whole range of topics related to Mennonites, but particularly historical, European, and North American.

Major popular periodicals of North American Mennonites include *Gospel Herald, The Mennonite, Mennonite Reporter*, and *Mennonite Weekly Review*.

The Editor

TED KOONTZ lives in Elkhart, Indiana, where he teaches ethics and peace studies at Associated Mennonite Biblical Seminary. His wife, Gayle, teaches theology and ethics at the seminary and served as dean, from 1990 to 1995. Their household includes teenage children, Rachel and Timothy, and a preteen, Peter.

Ted grew up in Kansas. He graduated from Bethel (Kansas) College, and received M.Div. and Ph.D. degrees from Harvard, focusing on ethics and on international relations. He worked in the office of Mennonite Central Committee Peace Section, Akron, Pennsylvania, from 1972-1976 and taught under MCC sponsorship at Silliman Divinity School in the Philippines, 1988-1990.

His favorite Scripture passage is Romans 8:18-39, which ends with Paul's vigorous affirmation that nothing anywhere "will be able to separate us from the love of God in Christ Jesus our Lord." His desire to know and to share that love inspired his work on this book.